AUGUSTO CURY

ANXIETY

HOW TO FACE THE EVIL OF THE CENTURY

*The Accelerated Thinking Syndrome: how and why humanity
has fallen ill collectively, from children to adults*

Translation to English: Elizabeth Ma Mendes

ISBN: 978-1-965965-08-5 (Paperback)

I dedicate this book to someone special

_____

I desire for you to be a great dreamer
And that among your dreams is having
A love affair with your quality of life.
Without this, you will be lacking much
From your emotional well-being and open mind.
Be aware that the best of human beings have already committed betrayal:
They sold their weekends, their sleep, their rest.
They betrayed the people they love the most by robbing them
of their presence. Slow down!
May you learn through this book how to
Manage your thoughts and protect your emotion.
For no matter how strong you are, you are a simple mortal.
Thank you for existing.

_____

___ / ___ / ___

ACKNOWLEDGEMENTS

Fortunately, women are taking over the world. In my opinion, they are more intelligent, altruistic and supportive than men. I thank the women of my life, my wife Suleima and my daughters Camila, Carolina and Claudia. From them I learned that every choice involves some kind of loss. Whoever is not prepared to lose the trivial is not worthy of achieving the essential. And if we are friends with wisdom, we will discover that what is essential are the people we love…

Table of Contents

Preface 1

1. The Evil of The Century: Depression or Accelerated Thinking Syndrome? 3
    What have we done to the sons of humanity? 4
    A mature or immature Self 6

2. Are Our Minds Free? 9
    Sartre's thesis: condemned to be free 9
    The Self is a hostage to a database 10
    The Self can be dominated by the autoflow phenomenon 12
    The ARM phenomenon controls memory and the Self 13
    Einstein's error and other consequences 15

3. Who Are We? Fundamental Theories 17
    Thinking is a great adventure 18
    Thinking and its traps 22

4. Stop, Observe Yourself, See Yourself! 25
    Statistics give us away 25
    ATS or hyperactivity? 26
    Life is beautiful and as passing as the dew 28

5. The Memory Trigger 31
    Vital anxiety 31
    Trigger or auto check phenomenon 32
    The memory trigger and its dungeons 33
    Traditional education 34

6. Memory Windows: The Information Storehouse 37
    Definition 37
    Personality shifts 37
    The willfulness of the Self does not change one's personality 38

Drug dependents...39

The dream is to build neighborhoods in one's memory 39

7. Types of Memory Windows 41

Neutral, killer and light windows 41

The Self walks on stage when the show is in full swing......................43

Examples speak louder than words 45

Reformulating the role of school 45

8. The Autoflow Phenomenon and The Self.................................47

A beautiful phenomenon..48

The Self and its fundamental roles 49

Functions of the Self as manager of thoughts 50

The mature or enslaved Self 54

9. The Self and The Autoflow: Partners or Enemies?.................57

The six types of the Self..58

There are no multiple personalities...63

The Self can have various sickly attitudes...64

10. The Accelerated Thinking Syndrome 67

Accelerated thinking...68

11. Murdering Childhood 75

It has never been so hard to educate 76

12. Levels Of ATS..79

ATS: disarm it! 79

Degrees of seriousness of ATS 80

13. Serious Consequences Of ATS 85

Premature aging of the emotion: chronic dissatisfaction...................85

Retardation of the emotion's maturity...87

Premature death of emotional life 88

Emotional defenselessness and the development of psychiatric disorders.......89

Other consequences of ATS 91

14. How To Manage the Accelerated Thinking Syndrome – Part I 93

1. Enabling the Self to be the author of its own story 93

2. Free to think, but not a slave to thoughts 95

3. Managing suffering in advance 96

4. Performing mental hygiene through the DCD technique 96

15. How To Manage the Accelerated Thinking Syndrome – Part II 99

5. Reprocessing false beliefs 99

6. Stop being a work machine: the most efficient patient in the hospital 100

7. Not being an information machine 104

8. Not being a traitor to the quality of life 105

Paying our "debts" and correcting routes 107

Bibliographical References 109

Preface

We live in a demanding, fast-moving and anxious society. People have never had such agitated, stressed minds. Patience and tolerance in difficulties are becoming luxury items. When the computer is slow to start up, many get irritated. When people are not engaged in interesting activities, they are easily annoyed. Few are those who behold flowers in the park or sit down for a chat on their porch or balcony. We are living in the age of the entertainment industry and, paradoxically, the age of boredom. It is very sad to discover that such a large number of people from every nation do not know how to be alone, to look into themselves, to reflect on the nuances of existence, to enjoy themselves or to carry out self-dialogue. These people know many other people on social networks, but rarely know anyone well, and even worse, they seldom know themselves.

This book talks about the evil of the century. Many think that the evil of the century is depression. Yet I present here another evil, perhaps a more serious but less perceptible one: anxiety resulting from the Accelerated Thinking Syndrome (ATS). Thinking is good, thinking clearly is even better, but thinking too much is a bomb against our mental health, our pleasure in life and our creativity. Psychotropic drugs are not the only things that cause addiction, but also information, intellectual work, activities, concerns and mobile phone use in excess. Are such excesses part of your life? They all lead the human mind to the most pervasive addiction: the addiction to thinking.

Many of the best professionals suffer from this evil. They are assets to their company, but tyrants to themselves. Decelerating our thoughts and learning to manage our mind are basic tasks.

The contents of this book comes from the Multifocal Intelligence Theory, one of the few theories in the world to study the complex process of construction of thoughts, the formation of the Self as the mental manager, the roles played by our memory and the production of thinkers. Therefore, this is not a self-help book, but a work of psychological application. I teach several of the theories mentioned here to my master's and doctorate students in Psychology, Coaching and Education Sciences. Nevertheless, I am attempting to write them in a simple language, using many examples and metaphors, in order to make this book accessible not only to many professionals, parents and teachers, but also to young people, who are ATS victims as well. Without realizing it, we have destroyed the emotional health of the youth all over the world. I hope you dive into the deepest layers of your mind and apply the tools proposed here.

Money can buy flatterers, but not friends. It can buy a bed, but not rest. It can buy tour packages, but not joy. It can buy any and every kind of product, but not a free mind. It can buy all types of insurance, but not emotional insurance. In such a short and complex existence as ours, achieving a liberated mind and having emotional insurance makes all the difference...

Dr. Augusto Cury, Ph.D

CHAPTER 1

The Evil of The Century: Depression or Accelerated Thinking Syndrome?

What is the evil of the century? Depression? There is no doubt that depression has reached an astounding number of people in modern society. According to the World Health Organization (WHO), 1.4 billion people, which corresponds to 20% of the planet's population, will eventually experience the ultimate stage of human pain. But as we shall see, the Accelerated Thinking Syndrome (ATS) probably affects over 80% of the population of all ages, whether students or teachers, illiterates or intellectuals, patients or doctors.

Without intention, the consumeristic, fast-paced and stressful modern society has changed something that should be inviolable - the rhythm of thought construction - which has produced very serious consequences to emotional health, the pleasure in living, the development of intelligence, creativity and maintaining social relations. We have fallen ill collectively. This is a wake-up call.

I recently applied a quick test on basic ATS symptoms to over eight thousand educators during two of my lectures, one being national and the other international.

I asked the participants to be honest and point out the symptoms they had. I mentioned that those who were not honest with themselves, who did not have the courage to look into themselves, ran the great risk of becoming

3

beyond reach and of carrying their conflicts to the grave. Before starting, I joked with them, telling them to smile, because it was a crying matter... The reaction amazed me, seeing that almost everyone was extremely anxious and presented psychic or psychosomatic symptoms resulting from this syndrome. They smiled and relaxed when they realized that they were not alone. They were victims of what I consider the true evil of the century.

What have we done to the sons of humanity?

After my last lecture, before catching my flight back to Sao Paulo, one of the event sponsors - the owner of a large educational institution ranging from elementary grades to college, with thousands of students - insisted upon my visiting his school.

I had twenty minutes. Seeing his great interest, I accepted. Since I did not just want to pay the school a visit, but to contribute somehow, I asked him to pick out a few classes of students to whom I could briefly speak about the complex functions of intelligence, the Self as manager of the psyche and how the Accelerated Thinking Syndrome jeopardizes the global development of the intellect. The teachers and coordinators quickly organized themselves and decided to choose the high school senior classes. I teach graduate students and professionals from different areas and I seldom have the opportunity to be with such young students.

I mentioned the killer windows, or traumatic windows – which I will talk about later on – that hold jealousy, shyness, phobias, insecurity and the feeling of incapacity, and which volume of tension can block off thousands of other windows, preventing the Self from accessing information and giving intelligent answers in a school test or in the tests of life. I told them that throughout history, many geniuses were considered "mentally retarded" by teachers who had never studied the memory windows theory or the killer zone traps hidden in the mind.

As I spoke to that audience, I was aware that young people around the world rarely pursue dreams such as that of Plato (the pleasure of learning), Paulo Freire (to have autonomy, one's own opinion), Jean-Paul Sartre (to create one's own destiny), Freud (an ego that experiences the pleasure principle with maturity), Viktor Frankl (a human being in search of the meaning of existence) and mine (the development of a mature Self, capable of protecting the emotion, managing thoughts and building up other complex functions of intelligence, in order to learn how to be the author of its own story).

Teachers complain that students are becoming increasingly agitated, anxious and alienated. But every mind is a safe. There is no such thing as an impenetrable mind, but the use of the wrong keys.

I used the correct key - I touched those students' emotional territory and motivated them to take a journey into themselves. Not a sound could be heard as I spoke.

After my brief presentation, I enquired if they might be experiencing any ATS symptoms. Most of them raised a hand, affirming that they had headaches and muscle pains. It was surprising. Almost everyone nodded when I asked if they woke up feeling tired, irritated and intolerant of difficulties, suffered before the fact, lacked concentration or had memory failures.

The perceptive school owner, as well as the teachers present, were startled. They had no idea that their students' quality of life was down in the dumps. Many students were wealthy, but lived miserably in the soil of their psyche.

Finally, I asked a last question. This time, I was the one with a trembling voice and tears in my eyes. I asked who had some kind of sleep disorder. Once again, many raised their hands. These young people were in the prime of life, but were stuck in the trenches, at war in the only place where there should be an absolute truce: in bed. Sleep is vital for a balanced, productive and healthy mind.

I stopped, looked at the teachers and asked, "What are we doing to the sons of humanity?" I could no longer restrain myself. I declared that although teachers are the most important professionals in society, the traditional education system is sickly and producing sickly people for a stressful society, because it teaches preschool to graduate students to acquire millions of bits of information on the world we live in, but hardly anything on the world that makes us who we are - the mind.

Traditional education rarely provides students with the basic tools for acquiring the ability to filter stressful stimuli, protect the emotion, manage thoughts, think before reacting and be resilient from early age, thus establishing the Self as mental manager and relieving, at least a little, the grave symptoms of the Accelerated Thinking Syndrome. Many schools in the Americas, Europe, Africa and Asia can skillfully produce experts, but are highly lacking when it comes to producing thinkers capable of developing free minds and healthy emotions.

Sadly, neurologists, psychiatrists and educational psychologists all over the world are misdiagnosing their patients. When they see an unfocused, irritable, agitated young person with a low frustration threshold, they diagnose hyperactivity or attention deficit disorder, instead of ATS. The symptoms are similar, but the causes and treatment are different. I will comment on this issue further on.

A mature or immature Self

We live in the Stone Age in regard to the role of the Self as manager of the psyche. How often do we take care of our physical hygiene and take a shower? Every 24 hours? What about our oral hygiene? Every four to six hours? What about our mental hygiene? For instance, how much time do we have to intervene when we are invaded by a disturbing thought, a self-punishing idea or a phobic state? Five seconds, at the most.

Using the metaphor of the theater, our Self, which represents our capacity of choice, should leave the audience, get on the stage of the mind and quickly and silently clean it up while the distressing experience is being registered in our memory. How? By refuting, disagreeing, confronting, just as a defense attorney protects a defendant in court. But our Self is far too slow. It is not trained to manage the psyche. It speaks out in the outer world and keeps silent in the mental territory. It usually does the opposite of what it should do.

Most people know how to drive a car, but have not learned how to drive their own emotions, reactions and thoughts. We live in a superficial and stressful society that sells us products and services daily. Yet it does not teach us how to develop a managing, mature, intelligent Self that is aware of its crucial roles. What is your Self like?

The psychic prison is headed by psychosomatic illnesses, depression, discrimination, school violence, difficulty in transferring one's wealth of experiences, the Closed Memory Circuit Syndrome, the Accelerated Thinking Syndrome, worship of celebrities and a tyrannical standard of beauty. Such prisons indicate that the management of the Self is in crisis.

I frequently comment with my graduate students in Psychoanalysis and Multifocal Psychology that one of the noblest and most relevant roles of the Self is to discover and scrutinize our ghosts and re-edit our traumatic windows. Otherwise, we will be part of that group that talks about maturity but are actual children in the emotional territory, who do not know how to take the least criticism or contradiction, in addition to having the neurotic need for power and for the world to revolve around them.

I once asked executives from the top 50 psychologically healthy companies in Brazil, "Which of you has some kind of insurance?" They all answered that they did. Then I asked, "Which of you has emotional insurance?" No one risked raising a hand. They were honest. How can we talk about healthy companies without mentioning the basic mechanisms for protecting the emotion? We insure only that which is dear to us. We have, unfortunately, given little value to our most important possession.

Generally speaking, these professionals were good to their companies, but tyrannical to themselves. They succeeded in what was trivial, but failed greatly in what was crucial. How about me? How about you? Even though we can say that the human mind is the most complex of all "enterprises" and the only one that must not go bankrupt, it unfortunately is the one that most easily fails, due to the inadmissible lack of attention we give to it. It cannot be treated as no man's land, left vulnerable to every kind of stressful stimuli. Does your emotion have insurance?

CHAPTER 2

Are Our Minds Free?

Sartre's thesis: condemned to be free

Are we free to think? Do we think whatever or whenever we want to? Wait, do not answer hastily. Think about thinking, think about what and how you think. Some may question this by saying, "I'm free in my mind, my thoughts are subject to my will." Is that really so?

French philosopher Jean-Paul Sartre defended one of the most intelligent theories in philosophy: the human being is condemned to be free. Was Sartre correct or was he being naïvely romantic in defending this thesis? Are we free within ourselves?

If we observe outward behavior, Sartre was undoubtedly correct. A prisoner's body can be confined behind bars, but his mind is free to think, fantasize, dream and imagine. If his Self is not trained to reflect on his mistakes, the penalty will by no means teach him anything. On the contrary, the phenomena that build streams of thoughts will make a multifocal reading of memory throughout the days, months and years, and build mental images of escape, tunnels, reduction of penalty; in short, everything possible to breakout from a prison that is worse than physical incarceration: the prison of anguish, of dullness, of asphyxiating anxiety. Those who built prisons throughout history did not study the process of construction of thoughts and did not understand that the mind can never be imprisoned.

Why do dictators fall, no matter how brutal or how much they control their people with an iron hand? Because no one can control the Self's activity and yearning for freedom.

Babies have the desire to leave their mother's arms to explore the environment. Adolescents venture to make new friends even though they may be shy. People that suffer from a phobia avoid the phobic object. In other words, they pursue their freedom. From this angle, Sartre was quite correct: man is condemned to be free.

So much so, that civil rights and responsibilities in democratic societies are founded on his theory, giving us the freedom to express our thoughts and to come and go. However, if on the one hand we desperately yearn for freedom, on the other, if we closely observe the process of construction of thoughts and its sophisticated traps, we will realize that Sartre's theory is naïve and romantic. Unfortunately, at the core of our intellect, we are not free as we would like to be. In fact, the worst prisons, the worst dungeons, and the tightest shackles may be inside us. Let's look into this.

The Self is a hostage to a database

We build thoughts from the body of information filed in our memory. All ideas, creativity and imagination come from the union of a stimulus with memory reading, which occurs in milliseconds. The Self is not aware of the high-speed data reading and organization that goes on behind the scenes of the mind. It is only conscious of the final product presented on stage, that is, the thoughts produced.

Paintings or even characters from a movie or book, no matter how uncommon, are created from the reading of elements in their authors' memory. And memory is a product of our genetic load, our mother's womb, the social environment, educational methods, and the Self's relationship with our own mind.

Thousands of experiences that make up our early childhood database, such as rejection, loss, setbacks, and fears were produced without our being able to control, filter or reject them. Today, as adults, we certainly make choices and take action, but our choices are based on what we have in our database. Therefore, we do not have total freedom as Sartre believed.

One man, who might have been the greatest educator in history, saw this limitation in a clear and marvelous way. When dying on the cross over two thousand years ago, he said something remarkable, ""Father, forgive them, for they do not know what they do!" An irreligious, psychological, and sociological analysis shows that this declaration conveys unprecedented altruism. But, at the same time, his attitude of protecting his executioners seems unacceptable.

The Roman soldiers knew what they were doing - they were carrying out Pilate's sentence of condemnation. However, to the Master of masters, the thoughts the soldiers produced were, on the one hand, the result of their free choice, and on the other hand, hostages of their memory's database and the Roman Empire's tyrannical culture. They were following orders. Neither were they completely autonomous, nor were they the choosers of their own fate. They were prisoners of their past, "slaves" to their culture.

Culture is essential to the identity of a people. But if it hinders us from putting ourselves in someone else's place and thinking before reacting, it becomes enslaving. To the Galilean master, behind a person who wounds there is always a wounded person. This did not solve his opposers' problem, but it solved his. It protected his mind. His Self did not carry the madness and aggressiveness of others. His tolerance brought him relief, even when the whole world was crashing down around him.

The Self can be dominated by the autoflow phenomenon

Our freedom is not just affected by our being hostages to our past and to "the freedom circumscribed to an existential history". Even within this database, we do not have complete freedom of choice as Sartre believed.

Imagine that we have millions of "building blocks" in our memory, which proceed from our genetic load, our relationship with parents, siblings and friends, school experiences, information from books, and the process of introspection. There is no doubt that we have the freedom of choice to use these blocks for building emotions and thoughts through the Self's own free will - accusing, reasoning, analytical, receptive, critical, accepting, loving and hateful thoughts.

Unless someone is having a psychotic break, is under the strong effect of a drug, or is a child incapable of being responsible for his actions, the exercise of choosing and using memory blocks is preserved. But despite the Self's freedom to access and use information to build chains of thoughts under its responsibility, unconscious phenomena build thoughts and emotions without the Self's consent. If these phenomena truly exist, our comprehension of who we are as *Homo sapiens* drastically changes.

Would you get on a plane knowing that there is a terrorist aboard who could take over the plane and make it crash? I asked an audience of doctors this question. Obviously, everyone answered no. Then I asked, "Who likes suffering and feeling distressed?" Happily, there were no masochists in the audience. I went on, "Who suffers in advance?" Almost everyone in the audience gave a positive answer. I then explained that if we considered the human mind as the most complex aircraft and the Self as its pilot, their mental aircraft would be in free fall. I said, "If your Self isn't masochistic, if you don't hate or try to maim yourself, why then do you suffer in advance? If your Self doesn't produce these disturbing thoughts, then who does? We can only conclude that there's a 'terrorist' on board, a co-pilot who's sabotaging the mental aircraft."

Who is this co-pilot? I call it the autoflow. Further on, we will study the autoflow in details, but in advance I affirm that this unconscious phenomenon is of vital importance to the human psyche, creativity and the pleasure of living. However, it can lose its healthy function and begin to terrorize us. In fact, it is greatly responsible for generating the Accelerated Thinking Syndrome.

Doctors have finally begun to understand that Jean-Paul Sartre's thesis did not support itself. Our Self is free to think and organize information in its memory, but, at the same time, unconscious phenomena that had not yet been studied by other theoreticians produce thoughts without the Self's consent and can sabotage, enslave, and imprison it.

We cannot say that we are condemned to be free. We are not alone on the mental, aircraft… We can and should be taught to be the author of our story, but this freedom has to be achieved and has its limits. The history of humanity with its countless injustices and atrocities is a clear example of this.

The ARM phenomenon controls memory and the Self

The third element that questions Sartre's theory is connected to the Self's limitations in regard to filing memory. When it comes to computers, we are gods - we save whatever we want, whenever we want. But this is impossible with human memory. The registration of everything we contact is automatic and involuntary. It is carried out by an unconscious phenomenon called Automatic Registration of Memory (ARM).

Not only what our Self desires will be filed, but also what it hates and despises. Everything we most hate or reject will be filed with more intensity, thus producing traumatic windows, which I call killer windows. If you hate someone, rest assured that this person will go to bed with you and ruin your sleep. Therefore, if the Self, which represents the capacity of choice, does not have the freedom to prevent disturbing thoughts and stressful stimuli from being registered, how can we say that man is condemned to be free?

Studying and grasping these unconscious phenomena will not only astonish us, but also give us a new understanding on education sciences, psychology, psychiatry, sociology and sociopolitical relations.

The process of construction of thoughts and all its psychological and sociological implications was not systematically studied by brilliant thinkers like Freud, Jung, Roger, Skinner, Piaget, Vygotsky, Paulo Freire, Nietzsche, Jean-Paul Sartre, Hegel, Kant, Descartes and others.

The great theorists of psychology and philosophy used thinking to brilliantly produce knowledge on the formation process of personality, the learning process, ethics, and sociopolitical relations, but investigated very little on that which can be considered the last frontier of science: thinking itself.

I spent over three decades thoroughly studying this area and developed the Multifocal Intelligence Theory (MIT). I thought day and night, year after year, analyzing and writing about the nature, types, limits and process of construction of thoughts.

This journey did not boost my pride. On the contrary, it put me in touch with my infirmities and smallness, making me realize, in over twenty thousand psychotherapy sessions and psychiatric consultations, that all my patients were as complex as the most educated and rational human being. Studying the dynamics, construction and activity of thoughts completely convinced me that every patient I treated, no matter how shattered the personality, had the very same dignity as I did.

We have the habit of classifying ourselves as black or white, rich or poor, renowned or unknown, educated or illiterate, kings or subjects, because we only walk on the surface of the psychic planet. At the most, we only know the entrance hall of the phenomena that shape us as *Homo sapiens*. We are a sickly species that has given little value to the art of thinking.

The fact that the most complex phenomenon of the intellect - thinking - has been so little researched has brought very serious consequences to the development of our species. Systematically thinking about the process of thinking causes us to break out of the prison of our own truths and opens a universe of possibilities for us to understand who we really are. It also helps us grasp that editing the construction of thoughts so frequently leads to the evil of the century (ATS) and to unprecedented brain fatigue.

Einstein's error and other consequences

Because we have not studied the process, types and nature of construction of thoughts, we have not developed tools for the Self to be a mental manager, which has generated some distressing paradoxes. Let's look into this. We have reached the pinnacle in medicine and psychiatry, but have never been so ill.

A recent study from the University of Michigan Institute for Social Research points out that one out of two people, that is, over three billion people, will, at some point in life, develop a psychiatric disorder. The entertainment industry is at its prime, but there has never been such a sad and depressive generation as ours. We are in the age of knowledge and of democratization of information, but we have never produced so many repeaters of information, instead of thinkers.

And the paradoxes go on. Because we did not investigate the basic phenomenon that makes us thinking beings, still today we experience the gross and very serious errors in maintaining human relations, including social inclusion. What is the difference between a person going through a psychotic break and an intellectual?

Were there any differences between the great Einstein and the psychotic son he left in the asylum, never again to visit? There were some differences in the organization of reason, parameters of reality, depth of ideas and configuration of imagination, but both were exactly alike behind the scenes of the mind.

Einstein's son built illogical thoughts and mental images disconnected from reality, but the Self's actions and the unconscious phenomena that built such thoughts and images were exactly the same as those used by Einstein when creating his sophisticated theory of relativity. Retrieving a verb from billions of options and using it in a chain of thought, even if an illogical one, corresponds to shooting at the moon and hitting a fly.

I repeat: the rapid memory reading and use of data that produced bizarre characters and ideas of persecution in the mind of Einstein's son were no less complex than that of his father. Nevertheless, the grim environment of an asylum, the difficulty to deal with his son's illogical reasoning, and his feeling of impotency led Einstein, the man who most knew the forces of the physical world, to suffocate with the forces of a more complex universe - the psyche.

When we study the process of construction of thoughts, we are enlightened to understand that insanity and rationality are closer to one another than we imagine. Therefore, an intelligent person never discriminates or belittles others.

CHAPTER 3

Who Are We? Fundamental Theories

A s I will talk about the Accelerated Thinking Syndrome and classify it as the great evil of the century, I feel the need to contextualize how I reached this discovery, in order to give more coherence to the following chapters on the causes and phenomena that ground this syndrome. The construction of thoughts is not linear, but multifocal. It does not only depend on the conscious will, that is, the Self, but on unconscious phenomena as well. This theory alone is already sufficient to prove that the human mind is more complex than postulated by psychoanalysis, behavioral theories, cognitive theories, existentialist theories, sociological theories, and psycholinguistic theories. We are so complex that when we do not have problems, we create them.

For example, millions of people in every modern society demand too much of themselves. They do not use thinking to free themselves, but to imprison and punish themselves when they fail or do not reach their expectations. Those who make excessive demands on themselves can be great for society and for their business, but they are definitely their own tormentors. Are you? We need to ask a relevant question. Is our Self the only phenomenon responsible for our self-punishment? The answer is no. Actually, because it is passive, the Self is muzzled by other phenomena that read the memory and close the window circuit.

Because the Self has not learned how the mind functions or to have self-control, it ends up being asphyxiated by unconscious engineers that build disturbing thoughts and punishments without the Self's permission. If we are not educationally equipped to act as managers of the psyche, we will be terrified children in a land of "monsters".

Of course, this does not exempt from responsibility those who commit violence against others. If the Self is aware and has not lost its parameters of reality, it is responsible for its behavior and consequences, including when it becomes a passive spectator of its mental illnesses. Those who do not give their emotion and thoughts a shock of lucidity will never be able to say that they are the author of their own story. We may never be completely free in our psyche, but there are different levels of imprisonment. Some visit this "prison" during weekly moments of stress. Others, in daily situations of tension. Still others constantly live in the dungeon.

Once, while I was lecturing at the Brazilian Federal Supreme Court, the guardian of citizen rights and responsibilities, the fortress of liberty, I stated that there have never been so many slaves in free and democratic societies in the only place where it is unacceptable to be a prisoner: our own mind.

It seems incredible to say this, but the time of slavery has not ended. It has only changed its address. Before, the body was in chains; today, the psyche is in chains. Before, slave drivers punished prisoners; today, we imprison ourselves. Before, working hours were inhumane - from 12 to 14 hours per day; today, due to ATS, our mental working hours are unbearable, for we have become thinking machines. We do not rest.

Thinking is a great adventure

The Multifocal Intelligence Theory (MIT) took decades (I am still writing about it) and over three thousand pages to be produced, in a country that gives little incentive to basic theoretical research, especially on the human mind. I would use my free time between psychotherapy and psychiatric consultations to write it, as well as precious hours on weekends, holidays, vacation, and in the evenings and early hours of the morning.

When we engage in a project to produce theoretical knowledge, we run the great risk of not developing anything consistent, especially in an intangible field such as psychology. But to win without risks is to triumph without dignity. The desire to contribute to humanity, even if minimally, drove me. Today, after so many years, and still putting myself in the position of an eternal learner, I am glad that this knowledge is reaching dozens of millions of readers in many countries. I also rejoice that some international universities have already offered master's and doctorate degrees in the MIT.

Yet it was an arduous task. It all started long ago and I now recall some peculiar moments. I met my wife in medical school. I was in my fourth year and she was in her second year. I had little resources, so I invited her for a cup of juice. As we were leaving, a note fell out of my pocket. She suspected that the note was from another girl, so she asked me what it was about. I looked into her eyes and told her that I was not very normal, for I dreamed of producing a new theory on intelligence, and that the paper was one of my notes. She found all this strange and must have thought I was delirious, with a passing fever, for as a future doctor I should be concerned with organs, sicknesses, treatments, and not with the functioning of the mind.

Time passed and my fever just got worse. Seventeen years later, another interesting incident occurred. I already had my three loving daughters. I was late for another social engagement because I was writing, and my wife was already in the car, honking the horn. When I got into the car, my oldest daughter, who was then 11 years old, asked me a fatal question, "Daddy, when are you going to finish your book?" I did not know the answer to that, and my wife, who at that moment was impatient, with every reason to be so, answered, "My dear, when I met your father, he soon told me that he was writing a book on the human mind. He's never going to finish it, because the day he finishes it, he'll die…"

* * *

It is hard to talk about my own production of knowledge. But never denying my great limitations, I would like to say that the Multifocal Intelligence Theory may have been the first to detect that the construction of thoughts is so complex that there are three other phenomena besides the Self that build chains of thoughts.

It is also one of the few theories to study the relationship between conscious thoughts and the nature of the object considered. Conscious thinking has a virtual nature, and therefore does not incorporate the reality of the object considered. What does this mean? Everything a parent says about a child, a psychologist about a patient, or a teacher about a student, never incorporates the mental or psychic reality of whom he talks about. This is why the MIT may be the first theory to demonstrate that, due to the virtual nature of thoughts, there is an antespace in interpersonal relationships. Due to this antespace, we are physically close to one another, but infinitely distant in psychic terms.

This paradoxal solitude (so near, yet dramatically distant), though unconscious, causes the Self and other phenomena to continuously produce thoughts, in order to bring together these worlds. Parents may be bewildered and sad to discover that they cannot reach the reality of their children's pain, joy, dreams, and nightmares. But this separation produces a crucial kind of anxiety that leads parents to unreservedly draw nearer to their children, to build bridges, talk to them, and want to be with them. In short, to break the bonds of solitude produced by the virtuality of thoughts. I think this is one of the most complex phenomena of psychology. The subject deserves an entire book.

Why do we never stop thinking, creating characters, imagining, producing a continuous film in our mind, not even while dreaming? It is not only because of our conscious will to think, work, and construct answers. There is something deeper, "down there", at the foundation of our psyche -

the unconscious motivation to reach the reality of people, environments and objects – that attempts to overcome the unimaginable solitude produced by consciousness. On the one hand, this process involves the construction of thoughts through vital anxiety, making us *Homo sapiens*, but on the other hand, it brings grave consequences, for a great part of our thoughts (diagnoses, analyses, judgments, and interventions) have little to do with others and a lot to do with ourselves. In other words, our thoughts are distorted and contaminated by our culture and personality (who I am), emotion (how I am), social environment (where I am), and motivation (what I intend). There are no pure interpretations.

No matter how impartial, people contaminate the construction of thoughts, even if minimally. It is impossible for doctors, psychiatrists, psychologists, judges, prosecutors, politicians, parents, and teachers to be completely impartial to the interpretive process, for the first action on the psychic stage occurs in milliseconds and not through the Self's action, but through two unconscious actors - the trigger and the memory windows -, still to be studied. Some interpretations do not seriously harm reason and are acceptable, while others are drastically distorted. This is why some judgments are political, based less on the law and more on the underlying and subliminal intentions of the one who judges.

Jealousy and the neurotic need to control one's partner - something so common to youth - are examples of distortions of reason in interpersonal relationships. Those who are jealous have already lost something: their self-esteem and ability to think clearly and calmly. A leading and mature Self neither gravitates around others, nor demands that others gravitate around it. It lives in harmony. Do you live in harmony with yourself?

Many adults criticize, exclude and put down others with attitudes typical to superficial and authoritarian people. According to the MIT, the virtuality of thoughts shows that absolute truth is always an unattainable goal. We should eternally pursue it. Those who believe they hold the truth are prepared to be gods, not human beings. Unfortunately, humanity is full of gods.

Thinking and its traps

Many psychiatrist and psychologists give limited and radical diagnoses for not having studied the traps that exist in the process of construction of thoughts. The diagnostics industry can be a problem. The same diagnosis that directs a patient's treatment can control, label and imprison him. Mental health professionals should know that they will never even minimally sense or feel a patient's pain of panic or depression. If they do, it will be their own pain and not the other's, for the interpersonal communicability occurs in the virtual realm and not through the transfer of essential reality. We are isolated in ourselves.

Many professionals from this noble and complex area do not understand that our knowledge of others always comes from ourselves. Learning to be as impartial as possible in the interpretation process and to criticize our prejudices is fundamental for drawing us closer to others and helping us understand their drama, even if only virtually.

Spiritual leaders, political leaders, jurists, and doctors commit serious mistakes because they believe that thoughts are instruments of truth. They judge, decide, condemn, and guide without knowing that the nature of thoughts is virtual. We should all be trained in college to understand the contamination (traps) connected to the nature of thoughts.

Our thoughts will never represent others in their fullness. Thinking with humility and recycling our authoritarianism, pride and neurotic need for power is crucial. Wars, genocides, homicides, violence, and bullying are not only produced by social factors, but also due to the fact that we have not studied the ambushes of the most complex psychic phenomenon: thinking.

How can we prove that conscious thinking is virtual, not concrete? It is simple. If it were not virtual, we could never think about the future, because it does not yet exist. Nor could we recover the past, because we cannot return to it. In the realm of virtuality, our species gave an unprecedented leap in the construction of imagination. However, we should keep in mind that the same phenomenon that freed us can also create great prisons, such as fear, hate, and dependence.

If parents, educators, and executives do not train their Self to empty out its prejudices and learn to put itself in the place of others in order to understand them as much as possible, they will make serious mistakes. Many become victims to envy, jealousy, anger, and the inferiority complex, unaware that such feelings are distortions related to the nature and construction of thoughts.

In addition to all these phenomena that I mentioned, the MIT studies dozens of other new areas of the psyche, such as the ARM phenomenon, the psychological adaptation phenomenon, the memory autocheck phenomenon or memory trigger, the memory windows, the three types of thinking (essential, antidialectical and dialectical), the Self as manager of thoughts, the Self as manager of the emotion, and the re-editing process of killer windows.

By systematically studying the conscious and unconscious phenomena that build thoughts, the MIT is the first theory to detect the Closed Memory Circuit Syndrome and the Accelerated Thinking Syndrome.

So far, I have briefly contextualized the construction process of the theory and some of its operational areas. I believe that from now on the chapters will be lighter. Producing a theory is a wonderful adventure, but has its lonely deserts. Those who dare to venture into spaces never before explored or to think outside the curve have a great chance of finding stones in their path. However, one is not worthy of contributing to science if one does not use one's pains and lack of sleep in this process. There are no skies without storms. Laughter and tears, successes and failures, applause and derision are all part of every human being's résumé, particularly of those who are passionate about producing new ideas.

CHAPTER 4

Stop, Observe Yourself, See Yourself!

Statistics give us away

To many, including doctors, lawyers, journalists, police officers, teachers, and employees, the mind is a great storehouse of disturbing thoughts. Surveys reveal that 80% of the young people in the world present symptoms of shyness and insecurity.

If we consider the Accelerated Thinking Syndrome as an anxiety disorder, it will be hard to find someone who is fully healthy in his mind. Humanity has taken the wrong path. We are falling ill quickly and collectively!

Are people who have ATS weak? By no standard! Do they lack intelligence? By no means! They have abilities like any other *Homo sapiens*, but they lack the capacity to protect their emotion and manage their thoughts. And are those who have depression and other disorders fragile? No! There is no doubt that metabolic factors like serotonin deficiency may be at the root of many depressive illnesses. Even so, despite these factors, if the Self were equipped to identify and disarm the mind traps, it would have a greater capacity to protect its emotional territory and be the author of its story.

This book does not replace clinical psychiatry or psychology, but serves as complementary material since it is a socio-educational psychology program for developing mental abilities.

ATS or hyperactivity?

As I said, many neurologists, psychiatrists, psychologists, and educational psychologists reach the wrong diagnosis when observing agitated, restless children and adolescents who have difficulty in concentrating and fitting into social norms. They attribute such behavior to attention deficit disorder or hyperactivity, when actually most of them are victims of the Accelerated Thinking Syndrome. Because they did not have the opportunity to research on the process of construction of thoughts, these professionals do not know that when we overexcite the unconscious "engineers" that build thoughts without the Self's permission, we easily develop ATS.

This disturbing syndrome produces some symptoms similar to those of hyperactivity, but their causes are different. Hyperactivity has a genetic background and often one of the parents is hyperactive. Moreover, the agitation and restlessness of a hyperactive person is manifested in infancy, while restlessness caused by ATS builds up gradually throughout the years. Among the causes of ATS are excess stimuli, toys, activities, and information.

Treatment also differs in some aspects. There is no metabolic alteration in ATS. The problem is functional and social, connected to the formation process of personality and functioning of the mind, and therefore should be corrected with certain techniques. Slowing down a child with ATS is essential. For instance, it may be quite helpful to encourage this child to develop calmer and more ludic activities, such as listening to calm music (classical music), playing instruments, coloring, practicing sports, or acting. Hyperactive children and adolescents can and should also perform these activities. Freely prescribing Ritalin and other drugs to those with ATS can be a serious mistake.

If both hyperactive young people and those who suffer from ATS do not learn techniques to manage their thoughts and protect their emotion, they will repeat the same mistakes, hinder their maturity, become irritable, present a low frustration threshold and have little capacity to adapt to difficulties, suffering from chronic dissatisfaction, besides jeopardizing intellectual performance. But what concerns me the most in ATS and hyperactivity is the retraction of two functions that are vital for social, professional and emotional success: thinking before acting and putting oneself in the place of others (empathy). It is crucial to develop these functions and this should be the goal of every school in every nation. Those who are concerned with their quality of life and their children and students' emotional health should study ATS at length.

We adults are unconsciously committing a crime against the emotional health of our young ones. My books are published in over sixty countries, not to bring me fame, which is fleeting and superficial, but to warn the scientific community and general population that in this fast-food society, where everything is fast and ready, we have dangerously altered the rhythm of construction of thoughts. How is your rhythm?

ATS hampers the process of elaboration of information as knowledge, of knowledge as experience and of experience as a complex function of intelligence, that is, thinking about consequences, proposing ideas instead of imposing them, putting oneself in the place of others, protecting the emotion, and especially managing thoughts.

Some young people only realize something is wrong with their lives when they become fragile, dependent, anxious adults, whose dreams have been buried in the alleys of history. Some parents only become aware of their family crisis after the relationship with their children has fallen apart, with no respect, affection or love. Some couples only realize that their relationship has failed after they have been through a world of misunderstanding. Some professionals only realize that they are unproductive, passive and uncreative after they have lost their passion for work and are deep in the throes of frustration.

We take our car into the shop just because of a simple noise that bothers us. However, our body screams out with excessive fatigue, insomnia, compulsion, sorrow, muscle pains, headaches, and other psychosomatic symptoms, and we still do not seek help. Do you hear the inaudible, the voice of your body and mind? Or do you only hear what is audible? Some only hear the voice of their symptoms when they are in a hospital, having almost been killed by a heart attack. Be smart and respect your life. Stop! Think! Observe yourself! See yourself! No psychiatrist or psychologist can do this for you.

Life is beautiful and as passing as the dew

We live life as if it were endless. But there is a short period of time between childhood and old age. Look back at your story: doesn't it seem like you fell asleep and woke up with your current age? The briefness of life stimulates superficial people to live destructively, without thinking about the consequences of their behavior, but invites the wise to value it as a diamond of priceless value.

To be wise does not mean to be perfect, not to fail, cry or have moments of weakness. To be wise is to learn to use every sorrow as an opportunity to learn lessons, every mistake as an occasion to correct one's path, and every failure as a chance to restart. In victory, the wise are lovers of joy, and in failure, friends of internalization. Are you wise? Do you look into yourself? Most of us are probably just acquainted with the entrance hall of our own personality.

One of the greatest complexities of psychology is to understand that the construction of thoughts is multifocal, not linear. According to the Multifocal Intelligence Theory, this means that we do not only build thoughts because we consciously accompany the Self's decision, but also utilize three other less conscious phenomena: the memory trigger (autocheck), autoflow and memory windows.

When we drive a car, we all have control over the accelerator, brakes and other mechanisms. Imagine us wanting to go one way and the car going another; we want to turn left, but the car of its own volition turns right. This astounding phenomenon constantly affects the vehicle of the human mind.

Our Self does not have complete control over the tools that build thousands of thoughts every day. This is why it is sometimes the protagonist; other times a mere spectator. It sometimes builds beautiful ideas; other times it becomes a victim to anguishing thoughts that it did not create. This intellectual dance between director and spectator, driver and passenger, manager and client, occurs throughout our story. This is why I affirmed previously that tragedy and comedy, laughter and tears, lucid reactions and stupid attitudes are all part of our résumé.

Let us once again use the metaphor of the theater to understand the human mind. The Self is or should be the leading actor on the mental stage, and the three unconscious phenomena that also build thoughts should work to make the Self shine. Yet these three supporting actors insist on stealing the show. The Self's greatest challenge is to leave its position of a shy spectator and take over the stage, playing its role as the manager of the mind. We need to face the evil of the century.

CHAPTER 5

The Memory Trigger

Vital anxiety

The phenomena that build chains of thoughts are continuously and inevitably moving in a constant flow and state of vital anxiety. Vital anxiety generated by the solitude of virtual consciousness is healthy, for it puts into motion the whole process of construction of the psyche, whether thoughts, ideas, characters, environments, desires, or aspirations.

Vital anxiety becomes sickly when it constricts the pleasure of living, creativity, generosity, affection, the ability to think before reacting, the capacity of reinventing oneself, and multifocal reasoning, among others. One of the mental mechanisms that most turn vital anxiety into asphyxiating anxiety is the hyperconstruction of thoughts. Those who have an agitated mind and have become an information and thinking machine have crossed the healthy boundaries of mental movement and will develop the Accelerated Thinking Syndrome. ATS is like a movie that has been edited at high speed. There is pleasure for the first few seconds, then it becomes unpleasant to the spectator.

According to the MIT, vital anxiety is a solemn testimonial that thinking is not just an option to *Homo sapiens*, but something inevitable. If the Self does not build chains of thoughts in a logical and coherent direction, unconscious phenomena will build other thoughts. Vital anxiety stimulates a dance of phenomena behind the scenes of our mind, even while we sleep. Dreams represent a reflex of this fascinating constructive movement.

Trigger or auto check phenomenon

The memory trigger is the first phenomenon to perform in the dance of unconscious phenomena that build thoughts. It is activated when we come into contact with extramental (light, sounds, touch, taste or smell) stimuli or intramental (mental images, thoughts, fantasies, desires, emotions) stimuli, and even certain organic stimuli (metabolic substances, neurotransmitter deficiencies, psychoactive drugs).

The trigger acts in milliseconds, without our Self being aware of its actions. It opens memory windows, activating immediate interpretation and instant awareness. At this exact moment, the reader knows who he is, where he is, what he is doing, his position in time and space, not because of the Self's conscious and programmed action, but because the memory trigger is anchored to hundreds of windows that support this instant perception. Have you never wondered about this process?

In a one-hour class or lecture, the memory trigger can be set off thousands of times to open thousands of windows for the immediate comprehension of each verb, noun, adjective, and pronoun. Every day, we see thousands of images that are quickly interpreted by the memory trigger and the subsequent windows it opens. This is why this phenomenon is also called memory autocheck.

Therefore, the first impressions and interpretations of the thousands of stimuli that we perceive are caused by unconscious phenomena, even though they become conscious. These actions occur during the first act of the mental theater. We do not grasp written and spoken words through a conscious, programmed and direct action of the Self, but through the pact between the memory trigger and memory windows.

If we depended on the Self to find each window related to the stimuli we receive, we would not have such a quick answer, we would not be the thinking species that we are. The action of the memory trigger is phenomenal. It checks the stimuli in billions of data stored in the base of memory with surprising quickness. You just read my words through the almost light-speed action of this magnificent phenomenon. Without it, the Self would be confused and would not identify languages, sounds and images from the most diverse environments. The reader would be missing.

The memory trigger and its dungeons

I once again repeat that without the pact between the trigger and memory windows we would not be a thinking species. However, this pact can also turn us into an imprisoned species. Every phobia, such as social phobia, claustrophobia, and acrophobia (fear of heights), is a result of this. Obsessions and drug dependence are also caused by the trigger, which immediately opens killer windows.

If on the one hand the memory trigger is a great helper to the Self, on the other it can be a great executioner. Due to the sickly windows it opens, it can lead to faulty actions or twisted, asphyxiating, superficial, and prejudiced interpretations.

Although those who have claustrophobia are not aware of the pact between the trigger and the killer memory windows, they know that this fear is cruel, though, without a doubt, it can be overcome. The tools I will present serve as a contribution to the psychotherapeutic process.

When a claustrophobic person walks into an elevator, the tightness in the chest, movement of the elevator or feeling of shortness of breath cause the trigger to quickly open killer windows that translate that the elevator will break and he can die. The volume of tension resulting from this window blocks the access to millions of bits of information, generating the Closed

Memory Circuit Syndrome. The Self then falls into a mental trap it did not foresee, which obstructs its clarity and coherence.

I had the privilege of discovering this syndrome and the unpleasantness of finding out that it is at the base of phobias, drug addictions, obsessions, depressions, homicides, suicides, wars, genocides, social exclusion, and even low intellectual performance.

Once, a brilliant student did badly on a test. He had studied and knew the subject, but he was nervous and could not remember the information, which caused him to do very poorly. The teacher criticized him. He was shook up and registered this frustration. He studied even harder for the next test. On the day of the test, the memory trigger came into action and opened a killer window that held the record of fear of failing.

The result? He became a victim of the Closed Memory Circuit Syndrome. He was unable to open the other files containing the information he had studied. He was extremely anxious and began to have very poor intellectual performance. Every time he took a test, the memory trigger and killer windows played their part. He was finally kicked out of college after years of failing tests. A serious action against his intelligence. Many geniuses are treated as mentally disabled because of these pernicious mechanisms.

Since many teachers and educational psychologists around the world are practically unacquainted with the pact between the trigger and the memory windows, they cannot help these students. In this particular case, the young man was only capable of overcoming, building up his self-esteem, recovering his brilliance in reasoning and doing well on tests when he learned to recover the leadership of the Self; in other words, when he learned to manage thoughts and protect his emotion.

Traditional education

The irony of destiny is not that it is inevitable, but a matter of choice. When the Self believes in this thesis and decides to take up the reins of destiny into its own hands, its personality is already built up and the "city of memory" already has well-defined centers of habitation. Tearing them down, reurbanizing and reorganizing them is a possible yet complex task. Just think of how complicated it is to remodel a house and you will understand how complex it is to rewrite our memory. Whoever has already renovated a house knows the trouble it involves.

Whoever has already gone through psychiatric and psychotherapeutic treatment knows that overcoming conflicts is not a quick process like going through surgery. But, of course, our hands are not tied, for we can recycle and re-edit traumatic windows, a task which requires techniques for the Self to become capable as the author of its own story and consequently demands a new agenda based on medium and long-term goals and priorities.

For example, imagine a person who suffers with social phobia and has a strong fear of speaking in public. One day, this person decides to turn the tables and fearlessly debate his ideas. His behavior is heroic and correct, but if the decision is made without surrounding support, it will only create solitary windows and not centers of habitation for the Self or a platform of light windows.

Sometime later, when he faces a new audience, that is, when he finds himself in a new stressful situation, there is a great chance that the trigger phenomenon will not find that one window that fostered his isolated courage among dozens of thousands of other windows. But the trigger will most likely find the countless killer windows that fostered his insecurity, fear of failing, and excessive concern with his social image. These windows may close up the memory circuit, imprisoning and silencing the Self, thus reproducing his social phobia. To overcome this, he should daily criticize and reprocess his fears and concerns. In this way, he will form a healthy center of habitation for the Self to be the protagonist of its story.

CHAPTER 6

Memory Windows:
The Information Storehouse

Definition

Memory windows are readable areas of the memory at a certain moment of existence. They are files to which the Self, the trigger, and the autoflow are anchored in order to read, use information, and build the most incredible phenomena of all: thoughts.

On computers, we have access to every field of digital memory. In the human memory, we have access to specific areas, which I call windows. A window is like a house. Each house has basic characteristics that define it, such as architecture, space, pictures, clothes, appliances. Similarly, memory windows have hundreds or thousands of bits of information that characterize them.

Personality shifts

In the book *Mind Traps*, I mention that willfulness does not change one's personality. At one time or another, we all have probably tried, without success, to change some sickly trait of our personality. Even psychopaths try to remake themselves at some point, but do not succeed. There is a consensus in psychology that one's personality cannot be changed. Actually, this consensus, which some consider a thesis, has no foundation or support. Personality is neither inflexible nor linear. It goes through a process of change, even if in the form of minor transformations. A personality shifts or transforms itself when the base of the memory windows is changed and when the Self is equipped to be its own leader.

Panic attacks, for instance, can very likely shift the formation of personality by creating powerful, imprisoning killer windows capable of building a center of habitation that hijacks the Self. A person who has presented panic syndrome (repeated attacks at least once a week) will never be the same again. He can become a better, more balanced, serene, altruistic person after he overcomes this syndrome, but the structural changes in his personality indicate that he will come out of the process different. A person who has been to war and experienced atrocities will come out of it with important changes to his personality.

The willfulness of the Self does not change one's personality

If personality is changeable, why then is it not easy to change sickly traits such as grumpiness, impulsiveness, a low frustration threshold, shyness? Because the intention or desire to change produces a solitary window, which is often a "poor" window with little resources.

A personality trait needs a center of habitation of the Self, a platform of windows, a whole "neighborhood" in the city of memory in order to be manageable and spontaneously located by unconscious phenomena such as the memory trigger.

A person is shy or outgoing not because the Self determines him to be so, but because there are thousands and thousands of windows spread throughout the fields of his memory. Likewise, an impulsive person has large platforms of windows in his cerebral cortex that are easily found and cause him to react so hastily.

Drug dependents

Drug dependents do not become imprisoned by the chemical drugs themselves, but by the filing of the experiences they have when using them. As time goes by, the problem is no longer the psychotropic substance, but the dungeon erected inside the Self, supported by the countless killer windows spread throughout the memory.

Dependents easily relapse, for even though they have had successful treatment, they actually have only re-edited a part of the traumatic windows that contain the representation of drugs. Other sickly windows remain "alive", capable of being found in the midst of a stressful situation and causing a new compulsion.

There is a false concept that a drug or alcohol dependent will be dependent all his life – this, in fact, is what Alcoholics Anonymous (AA) and many psychiatrists propose. But theoretically, it is possible to no longer be dependent. For this to happen, one needs to re-edit all the traumatic or killer windows, which is a difficult task since they may not appear during treatment.

Despite the concept (that a dependent will always be dependent) being false, it is useful for constantly keeping the Self in a state of watchfulness, for when the person faces a crisis, loss, or frustration the memory trigger will find sickly windows that have not yet been re-edited. If the Self is made aware of the mind traps and equips itself to be in control instead of punishing or destroying itself for having relapsed, it can use the situation to give itself a new chance, build more confidence, and rewrite the windows that trapped it.

The dream is to build neighborhoods in one's memory

Using the metaphor of a city, it is the neighborhoods, and not isolated houses, that define and represent personality traits. Most human beings carry the characteristics of their psyche that they most dislike to the grave because they do not establish an agenda to "reurbanize" the neighborhoods of their memory that have an open sewage system, poorly lit squares, streets full of potholes, and rundown houses.

These people do not know that although they have an effective desire to change, they are producing solitary windows that are inaccessible in stressful situations. Neither the Self nor the trigger memory can find them in order to give support to the desired changes.

Such people are always promising themselves and everyone else that they will change, become more patient, confident, proactive, generous, affectionate, and self-controlled. Some cry and despair, but remain the same. They do not understand that mental maturity does not require heroism, but human beings with intelligent humility, capable of recognizing their insignificance and immaturity and building up a new strategy, a platform of healthy windows, a new "neighborhood" in their memory. Heroism should be buried.

As we will study, man's great challenge is to open the maximum number of windows in a certain moment of existence to be able to reason with skill. However, if we find traumatic windows, unfortunately we will experience the Closed Memory Circuit Syndrome and prevent the Self's access to millions of pieces of data. This syndrome causes us to react instinctively, like irrational animals, thus making us victims of anger, jealousy, phobias, compulsion, with the neurotic need of power, of controlling others and of perfection. What strategy do you use to be the author of your story?

CHAPTER 7

Types of Memory Windows

Neutral, killer and light windows

Neutral windows

Neutral windows represent over 90% of all areas of memory. They contain millions of "neutral" pieces of information, which theoretically do not hold any emotional content, such as numbers, addresses, telephone numbers, school information, commonplace information, professional knowledge.

All existential information registered in the cerebral cortex from the dawn of fetal life to one's last breath is in these windows. We should ask ourselves a question: is all this information we have stored up spontaneously erased or replaced as time passes?

It is hard to say if the information is replaced or becomes inaccessible. Once the Automatic Registration of Memory stores thousands of pieces of information a day, millions a year, it is feasible that part of it is necessarily replaced. The "past" is reorganized by the "present", and the "I was" by the "I am". But most likely millions of data bits from the past which are electronically organized in the cells of the cerebral cortex are not stored in the conscious center, which I call Continuous Use Memory (CUM), but in the huge outskirts of memory, which I call Existential Memory (EM).

I am certain of this because when a person suffers brain degeneration, such as Alzheimer's disease, important areas of the CUM are disarranged or deleted. At the same time this intellectual accident occurs, the person is given access to information that previously was "almost" inaccessible, such as information from early childhood, which causes the patient to have memories and attitudes related to this period.

Killer windows

Killer windows correspond to all areas of memory whose emotional content is distressing, phobic, tense, depressive, and compulsive. They are traumatic windows or conflict zones. As the name itself describes, killer windows kill the body as well as the access to countless other memory windows, hindering or blocking intelligent answers to stressful situations.

When the trigger finds such windows – a phobic window, for example – , no matter how absurd the phobic object (a hummingbird or a butterfly), the volume of tension is so great that it blocks the access to thousands of windows, causing the Self to be imprisoned within itself, hindering it from giving a rational response. This is why even intellectuals can become unrecognizable when experiencing a panic attack, with disproportional, incoherent and illogical reactions.

Killer windows are windows that control, gag and asphyxiate the Self's leadership. There are several subtypes of killer windows, such as grumpiness, jealousy, anger, pessimism, impulsiveness, alienation, phobias, overconfidence, and dependence.

Some windows not only are traumatic, but also structural or "double P" which highjacks the Self. Double P means double power: the power to imprison the Self and the power to expand its own window or conflict zone; in other words, the power the make a person ill. Double P killer windows are built from extremely stressful stimuli, such as betrayal, public humiliation, panic attacks, or bankruptcy.

We should map ourselves out and ask which are the most important killer windows that rob us of our peace, our pleasure of living, our emotional health, our creativity, our self-control. We should bravely explore our psyche and inquire if we have double P killer windows that gag our Self and choke our emotional and intellectual abilities. We should all know that it is not possible to delete killer windows, but it is possible to rewrite them.

Light windows

Light windows represent all the readable areas that contain pleasure, serenity, tranquility, generosity, flexibility, sensibility, coherence, reflection, support, and healthy examples.

Light windows, as indicated by the name, "light up" the Self for the development of the more complex functions of intelligence: the ability to think before reacting, putting oneself in the place of others, resilience, creativity, complex reasoning, encouragement, determination, the ability to restart, protecting the emotion, managing thoughts.

The Self walks on stage when the show is in full swing

I am going to comment on something very serious about why we are a species that easily gets sick in its psyche and blotches up its story. The ARM phenomenon stores every experience we have had, whether pleasurable or distressing. It builds and fills memory windows that will be the foundation that supports and forms the Self, which, as we have seen, represents our critical consciousness and capacity of choice.

When the Self is relatively mature at the end of adolescence and, therefore, relatively capable of filtering stressful stimuli and writing its story, it is already a hostage to its past and to thousands of windows with millions of experiences. None of this can be deleted, only re-edited, which indicates the tremendous difficulty of changing the base of who we are. Finally, when the adult Self obtains critical consciousness as a unique being, the "city of memory" is already well organized with centers of habitation that already sustain the main personality traits, such as shyness, boldness, sensitivity, impulsiveness, emotional fluctuation, temperament, determination, insecurity, logical reasoning. Without a thorough education, the Self, in the fullness of its freedom, will live in a swamp! Take shyness, which affects about 80% of young people. The Self can reprocess it, but it is a more difficult process than the hardest physical surgery.

This is why we defend that the Self can and should learn, from the youngest age possible, how to use the tools to control itself. In other words, as the Self is being produced, it should also become a producer, and as it is being educated, it should also become an educator of emotion and a manager of thoughts.

Traditional education, from preschool to graduate school, teaches students multitudes of information about the world we live in, from the vast space to an atom, but hardly teaches anything about the mental planet and the phenomena that make us thinking beings.

This is why such an education, which formerly prepared people for life, is today, in this hypercompetitive society saturated with information, producing in general boys and girls with diplomas, who are without the emotional protection, the ability to deal with loss and frustration, or lack the minimum capacity to filter stressful stimuli and be their own leaders. Note that I am talking about more than just values. I am talking about the essential functions of the Self as the author of its story.

However, is this type of education the responsibility of parents or of schools? Both. We cannot ignore this. Both parents and educators have a responsibility for the emotional, social, and professional future of their children and students. Many parents outsource education, passing on to the school a responsibility which is also their own. This is an unforgivable mistake. Yet most schools dodge away from their responsibility in this process. I repeat: they take the time to transmit uncountable facts about the world we live in, but often keep quiet about the world which we actually are.

Examples speak louder than words

Probably over 90% of the influence that parents have in the process of forming their children's personality is not due to what they say, correct, or point out, but what they are and what behavior they spontaneously express, which is then photographed by their children's ARM phenomenon. When parents correct their children's mistakes, this forms a solitary light window, which only occurs if the correction is intelligent. But as we have seen, solitary windows do not structure personality or form centers of habitation of the Self. One needs a whole platform of windows.

Many parents lose their children's respect and the ability to educate because they do not comprehend that their children's spontaneous behavior will form a great part of these platforms of windows. Parents who want to teach their kids to be patient, but are impulsive themselves, or teach them to be flexible when they themselves are strict and inflexible, will have little success. Being an example is not just a good way to educate – it is the most powerful and effective way. Examples speak louder than words.

Reformulating the role of school

School should be a complement to family education, and for such, teachers need to know how to educate the emotion and develop the most important functions of intelligence to produce thinkers instead of repeaters of ideas.

Thinkers filter what they hear; repeaters of information obey orders and have a low level of critical consciousness and independence. Look at the case of pre-Nazi Germany. The Germans won one third of the Nobel prizes in the 1930s. The country had the best traditional education, excelling in Mathematics, Physics, Chemistry, and Engineering. However, this was not enough to purge Hitler, an uncultured, uncivilized and uncouth man, but one who was, at the same time, theatrical. When he showed up with Goebbels,

Himmler, Göring and others, and began his mass marketing, he seduced the young German population. The Self of the German people lost its autonomy.

It was a special situation headed by food insecurity, political fragmentation, high levels of unemployment (30%), humiliation, and heavy reparations to the winners of the First World War set by the Treaty of Versailles. A pool of killer windows controlled the collective unconscious of the German people, affecting their critical consciousness. Traditional education, though noteworthy, had not produced thinkers that collectively rejected or drastically filtered the mass marketing. A young German at that time dreamed, loved and dared as young people do today, but after years of being bombarded by the Nazi campaigns, his mind was so tamed that he was capable of killing a Jewish child for not taking off his cap in his presence, and a few minutes after, prepare himself to attend a musical concert.

As I mention in the book *The Tear Collector*, and especially in the psychiatric/historical novel *In search of the meaning of life*, Hitler and Goebbels firstly devoured the collective unconscious of the German people, then "devoured" Jews, Marxists, Slavs, gypsies, homosexuals and other minorities. I had the opportunity of discussing this subject with remarkable Germans in a Germany that nowadays is an example of respect to human rights. Who would imagine that the noble Germany of Kant and Hegel would be the protagonist of such an atrocity?

But the unavoidable question today is this: With the current traditional education that produces repeaters of ideas, is hooked on social networks, and directly affected by ATS, are we prepared not to repeat such atrocities when a new wave of killer windows, headed by global warming, food insecurity, and lack of natural resources strikes the collective unconscious of mankind? Unfortunately, my answer is "no". Producing thinkers and educating the emotion is vital and urgent.

CHAPTER 8

The Autoflow Phenomenon and The Self

The autoflow is an unconscious phenomenon of unequaled importance to the human intellect. The Self performs logical, directed and programmed reading of the memory, even though it sometimes presents distortions and lacks depth. Autoflow reading is different from that carried out by the Self. The autoflow performs an unconscious, random, unprogrammed scan of the most varied fields of memory, thus producing thoughts, mental images, ideas, fantasies, desires, and emotions. One of the great objectives of this unconscious phenomenon is to produce *Homo sapien's* greatest source of entertainment, distraction, motivation, and inspiration.

I will not go into details here, but besides generating the greatest source of human entertainment, the autoflow has another vital function: reading and giving feedback to memory windows from our mother's womb, in order to store millions of pieces of data for the development of thought in infancy. It was Freud who discovered the unconscious, or at least he was the first great spokesperson on the existence of the unconscious. Nevertheless, he did not have the opportunity to study the most remarkable unconscious phenomena of all – the autoflow, its rich functionality and its main roles. Freud discoursed on the pleasure principle as the main force of the psyche's movement. From babies to old people, we all hunger for pleasure, but the greatest source of pleasure is or should be the autoflow phenomenon. When this source fails, the consequences are grave and a state of unexplainable unhappiness takes over the mental scenery.

As an internal or intrapsychic source of recreation, the autoflow phenomenon daily takes us on a journey into our imagination, without any commitment as to the starting point, route or destination. Every day, each human being "wins" several "tickets" to travel through his thoughts and fantasies, sinking into his past and speculating about his future.

A beautiful phenomenon

Have you never been surprised with how creative our mind is? Even hermits travel in thought. No matter how isolated, monks cannot run away from the characters they create. Even though a psychotic patient has lost the parameters of reality, he still has a very fertile mind and creates ghosts that haunt him.

We are all engineers of thoughts, from the wise to the "insane". This is why to discriminate against human beings is intellectual stupidity. Moreover, the worship of celebrities is emotional childishness. We are all celebrated producers within our mind, even though some are experts at producing horror movies.

Notice the bubbling creativity in our dreams. Who is responsible for this? The autoflow phenomenon. It scans the memory, reads current and old windows, joining pieces at an incredible speed to creatively produce a cacophony of characters involved in the most fascinating adventures and environments. In this way, it keeps the flow of intellectual-emotional construction alive. The autoflow can be managed, but it can never be completely controlled; it is the greatest representative of vital anxiety.

Without the existence of the autoflow phenomenon, our species would develop serious tedium, collective depression, and a complete lack of existential meaning. As I mentioned, when this phenomenon fails to produce a source of pleasure and motivation, routine becomes asphyxiating, producing an anguish unexplained by social phenomena or personality traumas. Some people have good friends, children, a partner, financial and professional success, and plenty of reasons to celebrate life, but are grumpy and dissatisfied. What is the cause? The autoflow phenomenon does not have an intellectual-emotional production capable of inspiring them to sense the pulse of life as a remarkable spectacle.

In many cases, the starting point for the scan performed by the autoflow phenomenon are the windows opened by the memory trigger. For example, when a claustrophobic person steps into an aircraft, the trigger is pulled, opening a traumatic window that contains the fear of not being able to breathe or of the plane falling. Then the autoflow phenomenon anchors itself to this killer window and begins to produce an astonishing picture, construing hundreds of disturbing thoughts and causing the passenger to have an anxiety crisis (ATS) during small turbulences. And where is the Self in all this process? Paralyzed. If it reacted, if it confronted this mental horror movie as I will describe in the techniques for managing ATS, it would have a chance to be free.

Some executives confidently manage a company with thousands of employees, but are extremely afraid of flying. They go into a state of panic every time they have to travel by plane. Managing the human mind is much more complex than managing the greatest company in the world. We need educational tools and intelligent training.

It is surprising how easily the human being creates ghosts and anticipates its death. I hope you have not developed such an ability. If you have, your Self will have to learn how to pilot the mental aircraft skillfully and, for such to occur, it will have to stop acting as a mere passenger.

The Self and its fundamental roles

We commonly use the word "self" without understanding its dimension, abilities, and vital functions. The Self is the center of personality, the leader of the psyche or the mind, the conscious desire, the ability of self-determination, and the fundamental identity that makes us unique beings. As the definition of Self is broad and its main functions or roles are various, I will systematize them.

The Self has at least 25 vital roles. It is not enough for it to be serene, it needs to develop its crucial functions in order to honor its condition as *Homo sapiens*, a thinking being. Many professionals and intellectuals, including some who have doctorate and post-doctorate titles, have an unstructured Self and are intolerant to frustration. Although they are remarkably educated and praised by the academia, they are unable to deal with setbacks. They do not have the minimum ability to filter stressful stimuli and map out their problems. Their mind is no man's land and has no insurance. Is your mind protected?

I believe that most people from every nation and culture have developed at least 10% of these functions. While using the Multifocal Intelligence Theory to study these functions of the Self, I was disappointed with myself. Recognizing my insignificance, I reprocessed and positioned myself as an eternal learner.

Functions of the Self as manager of thoughts

I. To know yourself, map out your mental illnesses and overcome the neurotic need to be perfect.

II. To have critical consciousness and practice the art of doubting everything that controls you, especially false beliefs.

III. To be independent, learn to have your own opinion and make choices, but knowing that every choice involves some kind of loss.

IV. To have mental and social identity and overcome the neurotic need of power.

V.   To manage thoughts and classify them in order not to become a slave of ideas, which mulls over the past or anticipates the future.

VI.   To classify mental images and free your imagination to be intelligent in stressful situations.

VII.   To manage the emotion, by protecting it with the utmost authority, and filtering stressful stimuli.

VIII.   To overcome the neurotic need to change others (no one can change anyone) and learn to cooperate with them, surprising them.

IX.   To create social bridges: to know that every mind is a safe and that there are no impenetrable minds, but only the wrong keys.

X.   To learn to dialogue and share experiences, not just mention the trivial or pass on a manual of rules. Those who just use a manual of rules are only able to deal with machines and do not produce thinkers.

XI.   To reprocess instinctive genetic influences (anger, punishment, aggressiveness, and predatory competition) that make us *Homo bios*, in order to enrich the *Homo sapiens*.

XII.   To reprocess the influence of the social system that turns us into mere numbers instead of complex human beings.

XIII.   To re-edit killer windows, knowing that it is impossible to delete memory.

XIV.   To hold a roundtable with our mental "ghosts" in order to build parallel windows around the traumatic or killer centers.

XV.   To think before reacting and reason multifocally; to not be a slave to answers, but primarily true to your own conscience.

XVI.   To put yourself in the place of others in order to understand them more fairly from their own point of view.

XVII.   To develop altruism, solidarity and tolerance, including towards yourself.

XVIII. To develop resilience: to accept loss and frustration and reprocess conformism and self-pity.

XIX. To manage the principle of least and most effort: to know that the human mind tends to take the shortest path such as judging, excluding, denying, eliminating (law of least effort), but that maturity chooses a smarter and more elaborate path (law of most effort).

XX. To think as humanity as a whole and not just as a social, national, cultural or religious group.

XXI. To give the autoflow phenomenon a shock of management; to give it freedom as long as it does not anchor itself to killer windows or accelerate the construction of thoughts.

XXII. To manage ATS so that you are not just a thinking machine or a machine that wastes brain energy.

XXIII. To give a shock of management to the pact between the trigger memory and memory windows.

XXIV. To learn not to be a victim of the Closed Memory Circuit Syndrome and of the action-reaction phenomenon.

XXV. To be trained in all the 24 most complex functions of intelligence named above to develop the most noteworthy function of all: to be the author of your own story and manager of your mind.

My dream is that all the schools in the world – from elementary to high school – systematically teach these functions. My dream is that all universities, not just Psychology courses, include them in their curriculum throughout all courses.

Although, in my opinion, teachers are the most important and undervalued professionals in society, one of my cries of warning is that the world educational system is dying, producing immature students who are unprepared to be their own leaders in a digital society. The system dumps millions of bits of data about the objective world on its students, but does not systematically teach the functions of the Self in the subjective world. What should they do with derision and shame, challenges and frustrations? What about tears, betrayals, or the ghosts lodged in the unconscious? How should they map out the psyche? How should they reprocess their neurotic needs? How should they slow down and clean their minds? How should they disarm killer windows? They do not know any of this. When they get something right, it is by mere intuition, for they have not been trained to manage the mind.

After hearing my lecture on what goes on behind the scenes of the mind, a German expert in social communication publicly declared, "I don't have killer windows. I am a killer window. Unfortunately, I've never learned to re-edit them and have always tried to delete my memory. I used mechanisms that never worked."

Once I was invited by the Brazilian Marine Corps to speak to their leading marines about the Multifocal Intelligence Theory and the formation process of thinkers. After my talk, a brilliant admiral commented, "Our marines are experts in naval, chemical, and mechanical engineering; in other words, they're experts in dealing with logical data. But our resumes need to be updated in order to include the development of the Self and its vital functions. We need to learn how to deal with the difficulties of life, with social and emotional conflicts, and above all, learn to make intelligent decisions in risky situations." He had fully grasped the content of my lecture.

On another occasion, a young college student came to me saying that her mother had committed suicide a couple of months before. Her world had fallen apart. She could not look anyone in the eye and was downhearted and depressed. She never left the house and abandoned her studies, shutting herself up in a dungeon. She considered herself the loneliest person on Earth. She mentioned that her relationship with her mother had been great, but that the connection with her father was distant and full of conflict. Her father had been unfaithful to her mother.

She also told me that several people in her family had committed suicide. I was worried that she would follow the same path, being that she was depressed, distressed, and lacking the vital functions of the Self to manage her psyche. I encouraged her to seek treatment and told her that over ten million people per year tried to commit suicide and that, sadly, one million were successful. But I also mentioned that her mother did not want to put an end to her life, just an end to her pain. I told her that she should not be angry at her mother for abandoning her and explained the psychodynamic mechanism of suicide to her.

Her mother had been a victim of the Closed Memory Circuit Syndrome. She had opened stressful windows connected to self-abandonment, feelings of exclusion, resentment, and depression, which block the access to thousands of other windows, causing her Self to react by instinct without thinking.

I told this girl that she should develop some vital functions of intelligence. She should hold a roundtable with the Self every day to fight everything that controlled her, manage her thoughts, give her emotion a shock of lucidity, re-edit her memory windows, and transform chaos into a creative opportunity. She understood that she could either be a conformist, a victim to the world, or the protagonist of her story. She smiled, which she had not done in a long time, and said that she would daily use the techniques I had offered her to train her Self and learn to be the author of her own story. I rejoiced for her.

The mature or enslaved Self

In traditional education, the Self is not organized, trained or equipped to be the mental manager. It becomes an accomplisher of tasks, intentions and desires. "I do, I did, I will do", "I wish for, I wished for, I will wish for". At the most, this Self will develop critical consciousness and identity. But over twenty of its vital functions will remain untouched. It is an immature, enslaved Self, subject to obeying orders without being aware of its essential functions and, therefore, incapable of being the manager of the mind, pilot of the mental aircraft, or producer of its own story.

What do we do when we are betrayed, wounded, slandered, rejected? Do we write the most important chapters of our story or the worst texts of our memory? Are we victims of the Closed Memory Circuit or do we protect our mind so that we do not sell our peace and emotional health at a worthless price? Sadly, we overthink the stressful stimulus and stimulate the ARM phenomenon to produce countless killer windows, building up a traumatic nucleus, a center of habitation that hijacks the Self.

The education that does not broach the most complex functions of intelligence brings serious consequences to psychiatry and psychology, by fomenting the production of mental disorders, to education itself, by stimulating the formation of repeaters of information instead of thinkers, to political sciences, by promoting corruption, selfishness, egocentrism, and the neurotic need for power, and to the evolution of our species, by fostering irrational disputes, political and religious fundamentalism, fragmentation of mankind, and long-term unviability.

If a person possesses a healthy and intelligent Self with well-developed vital functions, he will have substantial consciousness of himself and of the complexity of his psyche, never making himself inferior or superior to others. He may stand before the president or the king of his nation without belittling himself or having the impulse to over-esteem them. He may have consideration and respect for them, but not irrational fascination. Most young people who are fascinated by Hollywood or music celebrities do not have an independent, self-aware and self-critical Self.

A healthy and intelligent Self realizes that all human beings are equally complex in the process of construction of thoughts, although this construction has different cultural manifestations, reasoning speed, coherence, and sensibility.

CHAPTER 9

The Self and The Autoflow: Partners or Enemies?

A healthy and intelligent Self sees the greatness of existence. It knows that human beings are like "children", in a good sense, who "play" in the theater of time, buying, selling, relating to others, surrounded by an ocean of secrets that surpass the boundaries of their understanding.

A healthy and intelligent Self sets its social agenda on flexibility, the ability to propose thoughts instead of imposing them. Those who impose their ideas, whether through a loud tone of voice, social pressure, financial pressure, excessive demands, or unending sermons, are not authors of their own story or producers of thinkers, but servants – passive, intimidated and subservient.

Many leaders have never been worthy of their power, for they do not know how to liberate the intellectual potential of those they lead. They asphyxiate and do not supply the necessary oxygen for others to express their ideas and be creative, proactive, enterprising. They have the need to be the center of attention. Such people do not deserve praise if they love themselves more than the people they lead.

A mature Self is self-aware, determined, and firstly its own leader before it leads others. Among its activities, a mature Self gives a shock of intelligence to the construction of thoughts carried out by unconscious phenomena, especially the autoflow. Let's look into this.

The six types of the Self

The managing Self

These are the people whose Self has learned to manage its thoughts and practice the art of questioning itself. Such people know how to set their imagination free, appreciate the movement of the autoflow, are creative, motivated and inspired, and capable of criticizing their ideas, truths and beliefs.

They know that those who overcome without difficulties triumph without greatness. Therefore, they break the bonds of monotony, journey into the unknown, are curious, and seek that which is over the horizon. At the same time, their Self has the maturity to reprocess and classify thoughts and mental images. They are aware that the autoflow phenomenon is a source of inspiration, entertainment, and adventure, yet do not allow themselves to be controlled by it.

The managing Self takes daily care of its mental hygiene: it questions disturbing thoughts, criticizes false beliefs, and strategically determines or decides where it wants to get to; therefore, it uses the doubt, criticize and determine technique (DCD).

The managing Self is carefree, turns chaos into a creative opportunity, possesses the resilience to use pain to grow, acknowledges its mistakes, apologizes, and captivates people, for it does not have the neurotic need to be perfect. This is why this type of Self is capable of speaking of its sorrows to children and students so that they can learn to shed their own tears. Because one day they will.

The traveling or disconnected Self

These are the people who let their Self embark on every journey offered by the autoflow, unrestrained by any management. Emotional heaven and hell are very close for those with a disconnected Self. Such people have not lost the parameters of reality, they have not had a psychotic breakdown, but since they are traveling in their own mind, they easily alternate between happy and stressful moments.

Once the traveling Self does not have the minimal management of its mind, depending on where the autoflow is anchored in the memory, those with this type of Self will be passive spectators of the thoughts, ideas, mental images, and emotions built by this unconscious phenomenon. A disconnected Self does not take control of its own story. Wherever the autoflow roams, the Self naively follows.

People with a disconnected or traveling Self are always submerged in their mind, thinking, wondering, fantasizing. They are so distracted and unfocused that you may talk to them for several minutes without them paying attention to anything you say.

Many smart people, including geniuses, have a traveling Self. However, because they are disconnected from reality, they unfortunately do not use their intellectual potential adequately.

They are dreamers, but do not have the discipline to transform their dreams into reality. They are great at speaking, but unproductive. They love applause, but do not like to tune the piano, carry it or play it.

Many people with a disconnected Self are affectionate, generous, and calm. But in many cases, selfishness and egocentrism are at the foundation of this disconnection. Few are concerned with the pain of others and due to this have no urge to relieve it. Learning the art of altruism and observation demands daily practice for the disconnected Self.

Some students have such strong ATS and are so disconnected when in the classroom that I have them use the following technique in order to concentrate and improve their intellectual performance: make a quick mental summary of what the teacher is saying in class and quickly write it down.

The drifting Self

The drifting Self, just as the disconnected Self, has no anchor, security, stability, or clarity of where it is and where it wants to go. It follows the random movements of the autoflow phenomenon as it reads the memory. It is not even capable of intuitively giving direction to ideas, thoughts, goals, and projects. People with a drifting Self do not exercise their capacity of choice. They have no autonomy, ideas, or intellectual guidelines. One moment they have an opinion. The next, they are influenced by others or by the environment. They change their mind easily. Given a situation, they may dream up something, but in the heat of a problem, they give up and change their direction.

The drifting Self is unstable, which therefore unbalances the emotion to become voluble and adrift. This is why people with this type of Self are happy one moment and sad the next. They are motivated in the morning, languid in the afternoon, and just want to sleep at night because they have lost their "momentum". One minute they are affectionate, the other irritable and even aggressive. Drifting executives cause their employees to walk on thin ice. In extreme cases, they wither their workers' spontaneity, creativity, and pleasure of working in the company, for the employees never know what mood their boss will be in.

People with a drifting Self disturb their own relationships and trouble their partner's, children's, and friends' peace and pleasure. Managing their mood and acquiring emotional stability are the main goals of those who have a drifting Self.

The rigid Self

These are the people who do not release the autoflow phenomenon and, consequently, restrain their imagination and creativity. Their Self is rigid, closed, and inflexible. Such people have great creative potential, but are hard on themselves. They do not dream, feel inspired, and are afraid of opening up and thinking about other possibilities. They are constantly bored and bore those around them.

A rigid Self radically defends its political party, convictions or religion and therefore does not give itself space to respect what is different. Those who are radical are not convinced about what they believe in, for if they did they would not have to pressure others when expressing themselves. On the other hand, those who radically defend their atheism are emotionally immature, for they need to use coercion to uphold their own convictions.

A rigid Self is like a mental robot. It wakes up the same way, complains about the same things, gives the same answers, and has the same attitudes when the same problems. Such a person is imprisoned by routine. He may even have many reasons to be grateful for life, work, and family, but wallows in a swamp of complaints. Do you know anyone like this?

These people may even be successful outwardly, but are miserable inwardly. Their greatest source of entertainment is impaired and depleted. Their Self enjoys anchoring itself to killer windows that foster pessimism, dissatisfaction, irritability. Training our capacity to change whenever necessary, thinking about other possibilities, self-criticism, and acknowledging our inflexibility are very intelligent attitudes to remove our mental rigidity.

The self-sabotaging Self

The self-sabotaging Self does not manage the process of construction of thoughts to promote emotional stability and depth. As amazing as it may seem, this type of Self works against freedom and conspires against one's pleasure of living, peace, professional and social success. People with a self-sabotaging Self are their own executioners. A Self with these characteristics desperately needs to learn to love its qualities.

Thousands of overweight women have a self-sabotaging Self. They go on diets, struggle to lose weight, and after much effort succeed. However, they are unable to maintain their weight loss or rejoice in their victory because the autoflow phenomenon anchors itself to killer windows that produce self-punishment. The fragile Self then surrenders to these traumatic zones with the consequence that it neither allows itself to feel good or happy nor will it accept compliments. Success stresses out such people. They begin to sabotage their diet and to eat impulsively. They only seem to feel alive if they are punishing themselves. They often give up on their dreams along the way.

The self-sabotaging Self does not know how to apply a shock of management to the autoflow, which apart from self-punishment, also carries phobias, obsession, dependence, jealousy, envy, and anger.

A person who sabotages his emotional health is always terrorizing and tormenting himself with facts that have not occurred yet, endlessly circling past problems, and regretting loss, failure and injustices.

A Self who sabotages its own happiness can be good to others, but horrible to itself. It can be tolerant with close ones and friends, but implacable towards itself. It can give chances to others when they make mistakes, but rarely gives itself a second chance.

One of the most grave personality defects of a self-sabotaging Self is that it is too self-demanding. Unfortunately, as a great number of people have this sickly characteristic, I will reinforce what I have already said. Those who demand too much of themselves use up the oxygen of their own freedom, choke down creativity, and what is worse, stimulate the automatic registration of memory to produce killer windows every time they fail, stumble, fall down or in any way do not meet their high expectations.

An important warning: one of the most serious consequences suffered by those who demand too much of themselves is to raise the levels of demand, which prevents them from relaxing or feeling accomplished, satisfied and happy. Those who make much out of little are much more stable and healthier than those who need a lot to enjoy a few crumbs of pleasure.

The self-sabotaging Self causes many successful professionals to fail emotionally. They sabotage their vacation, weekends, holidays, sleep, and dreams.

The accelerated Self

The accelerated Self belongs to the large group of people all over the world and in every modern society, from children to the elderly, who clutter themselves with information, activities, and preoccupations. Consequently, they stimulate the autoflow phenomenon, causing it to produce thoughts at a speed never seen before, thus generating the Accelerated Thinking Syndrome.

ATS has become the evil of the century and produces terrible quality of life, chronic dissatisfaction, the retraction of creativity, psychosomatic diseases, interpersonal relation disorders, and especially disorders in the way the Self relates to itself.

There are no multiple personalities

We should bear in mind that the Self can present different attitudes within the same personality. Multiple personalities do not exist, as some people believe, including psychology professionals. What do exist are distinct centers of habitation or memory platforms to which the autoflow and the Self anchor themselves.

Some people change their tone of voice and react so differently from usual that it seems like two or more people live in the same brain. What actually happens is that the Self feeds on information and experiences from the platform the autoflow is anchored to, in order to produce thoughts and emotions, thus revealing traits belonging to the personality.

Some people are calm when anchored to a certain center of habitation, but become stupid when not attached to it. Some people are strong and secure in a certain situation, but feel intimidated, like a child before a beast, in a different one. If the platforms are qualitatively different from one another, their characteristics will also be distinct.

The Self can have various sickly attitudes

A person can have an accelerated Self and, to worsen his emotional health, can also have a rigid, self-sabotaging or disconnected Self. In other words, besides the person being restless and agitated, he can also be inflexible, emotionally unstable, and at the same time, his worst enemy and own executioner, pessimistic and grumpy.

Even when the Self's posture reveals levels of creativity, maturity, resilience, the ability to adapt to changes, protection of the psyche and the capability to overcome conflicts, we cannot forget that in psychiatry and psychology nothing is unchangeable. The human psyche can go through a process of transformation, especially if the Self reprocesses itself and becomes a builder of platforms of light windows, that is, a constructor of new centers of habitation in the cerebral cortex.

One of the theses I defend in the book *The fascinating construction of the Self* is that, in the metaphor of a city, a human being does not need the entire city of memory to be perfect, free of potholes, open sewage systems or traumatized neighborhoods, in order to live a dignified life.

Just like in a physical city, if you build healthy centers of habitation, it is possible to live an acceptable and pleasurable life. If it were not so, the formation process of personality would be completely unfair. Children who were sexually abused, deprived of minimal living conditions, socially humiliated, or mutilated in wars and terrorist attacks would not be allowed the chance to have a free mind and healthy emotion.

We are gods on the computer because we save and delete what we want whenever we want, but this is impossible with human memory. Nevertheless, this does not mean that we are condemned to live with our mental illnesses.

We can take hold of all the roles of the Self that have been listed, and consequently re-edit memory, making use of certain tools, such as the DCD technique, the roundtable of the Self, the protection of the emotion, and resilience to begin to direct our own story.

However, we should never forget that magical solutions do not exist in psychiatry, psychology, sociology, and education sciences. One must establish a new agenda to build centers of habitation of the Self. This requires daily educational exercises. We should always keep this thesis in mind: if society abandons us, solitude is treatable, but if we abandon ourselves, it is practically incurable.

CHAPTER 10

The Accelerated Thinking Syndrome

In previous chapters, I mentioned some mechanisms of the process of construction of thoughts. Therefore, the ground has been prepared for me to speak more specifically about the great evil of the century: the Accelerated Thinking Syndrome.

Just as I had the privilege of discovering the Closed Memory Circuit Syndrome, which is at the base of domestic aggression, bullying, professional conflicts, suicide, wars, and other forms of violence, I also had the pleasure of unveiling the most penetrating and "epidemic" syndrome that affects modern societies: the Accelerated Thinking Syndrome.

At the same time, however, I had the disappointment of finding out that different levels of this syndrome affect a great number of people from almost every age group, including children, who are treated either as geniuses or as hyperactive individuals. We are destroying their childhood without realizing it.

Thinking is good, thinking with critical consciousness is even better, but thinking in excess is a bomb against quality of life, a balanced emotion, a creative and productive intellect.

Accelerated thinking

Not only is the pessimistic content of thoughts a problem that affects the quality of life, but what we did not know is that the exaggerated speed of these thoughts is also an attack against its quality. Editing or accelerating thoughts without control is the most evident sign that the Self is failing as a mental manager. No one can tolerate watching a movie in fast-forward mode for very long. Yet, for years, we have watched the "movie" played by our thoughts, which brings serious physical and mental consequences.

The Accelerated Thinking Syndrome and its causes, symptoms, consequences, and methods to overcome it should be included in the curriculum of every school, from preschool to graduate school. But we do not have the time to explore the world that transforms us into thinking beings. "Informative" education stresses out the best teachers and their students. And to make things worse, it harms creativity and emotional health.

Any layman knows that a machine cannot work at high speed continuously, day in day out, because its temperature will rise, causing parts to melt down. But it is almost unbelievable that we human beings do not have the least awareness that thinking in excess and without any self-control is a source of mental depletion.

Children and adolescents are mentally exhausted. Parents and teachers are fatigued without knowing the cause. Professionals from the most diverse fields wake up without energy and have to drag themselves around all day.

Once, I was in Orlando speaking to my master-degree students from over thirty countries about ATS symptoms. They were astonished and most of them realized that they needed to rest for a long period. They urgently needed to train their Self to manage their thoughts, change their life style, and learn to value their mental health.

Humanity has taken the wrong turn. We are quickly, intensely and globally become stressed in an age of computers and Internet. We are pushing the psyche into a state of collective failure, and we are unaware of this evil of the century.

Even if the content of our accelerated thinking is positive, cultured, or interesting, the acceleration itself generates intense brain fatigue, which produces the most important anxiety of modern times with the greatest wealth of symptoms. We do not need to have a sickly childhood to become anxious adults; all we need to fall ill is to have an overaccelerated mind.

There are many kinds of anxiety such as post-traumatic stress, obsessive compulsive disorder (OCD), burnout syndrome, and panic disorder, but the anxiety produced by ATS is more comprehensive, continual, and "contagious".

I have listed some ATS symptoms below:

I.	Anxiety
II.	Restless or agitated mind
III.	Dissatisfaction
IV.	Severe physical fatigue; waking up feeling tired
V.	Suffering in anticipation
VI.	Irritability and emotional fluctuation
VII.	Impatience; everything has to be done quickly
VIII.	Difficulty in enjoying routine (tedium)
IX.	Difficulty in dealing with slow people
X.	Low frustration threshold (little problems cause great impacts)
XI.	Headaches
XII.	Muscle pain
XIII.	Other psychosomatic symptoms (hair loss, tachycardia, high blood pressure, etc.)
XIV.	Lack of concentration
XV.	Memory losses
XVI.	Sleep disorder or insomnia.

Although there is no rigid classification, empirically, we can say that those who have at least three or four of these symptoms should quickly change their life style. Take a test to assess your quality of life at www.augustocurycursos.com.br.

One of the marking characteristics of the Accelerated Thinking Syndrome is suffering in anticipation. We suffer beforehand from facts and circumstances that have not yet even occurred, but which are already prepared in our mind. Even those who hate horror movies often create a ghostly movie in their mind. Their Self sabotages their peace.

Without knowing the reason, every teacher in the world acknowledges that since the end of the twentieth century, children and adolescents have become more and more agitated, restless, lacking in concentration, the respect for others and the pleasure in learning.

Why do so many wake up feeling tired? Because they spend too much energy thinking and worrying in their sleep. Sleep is no longer restorative; it is incapable of restoring energy at the same speed.

And why do these physical symptoms appear? When the brain is worn out, stressed, and without energy, it looks for means of shock to warn us. This is why a series of psychosomatic symptoms such as headaches and muscle pains appear. They represent the wake-up call of billions of cells begging for a change in our life style. But who listens to the voice of his own body?

What about forgetfulness? Why have we been a population who suffers from memory deficit? Because our brain has more good sense than our Self. Our brain realizes that we do not know how to manage our thoughts and that we are always fatigued, so it uses instinctive mechanisms to block our memory windows in the attempt to make us think less and conserve more energy.

In education conferences, I frequently ask the teachers if they suffer from memory deficit. The answer is always the same: most of them say "yes". Then I warn them in a joking tone, but being serious. "Dear teachers, if you are collectively forgetful, how then can you have the courage to require that your students remember the subject while taking tests?" Many laugh and clap. But deep down, I am not joking. I am pointing out something very serious.

Our students also suffer from ATS, which hinders the absorption, organization and retrieval capacity of information, and affects the performance of reasoning. Brilliant students no longer shine in tests, not because they do not know the subject, but because they have short-circuited this process.

I have affirmed that the ministries of Education and Culture in many countries are wrong to evaluate a student by getting answers right in tests. Students should not only be evaluated for their capacity of data repetition, but for their inventiveness, logical reasoning capacity, and boldness. Moreover, if we want to produce thinkers, we need to evaluate students outside the environment of tests, in the classroom, observing their interactivity, altruism, proactivity, discussion of ideas, discourse, and social cooperation. These elements are what determine professional and social success in the test of life, much more than getting the answers right in school tests.

Memory deficit affects all types of people at various levels. Some people are so forgetful that they even have a hard time remembering the names of their work colleagues, where they put the car key, and where they parked. Daily forgetfulness is the brain's positive warning that the red light has come on and that ATS has asphyxiated our mind to the point of seriously harming our quality of life. Daily memory deficit is a brain protection, not a problem, as many doctors deem it.

I repeat: the brain blocks off certain memory files, attempting to decrease the excess thoughts produced by ATS. A stressed person who suffers from ATS can spend more energy than ten blue-collar workers put together. Wise are those who produce much consuming very little energy.

What is the use of being a work machine if we lose those we love most, and if we do not live a peaceful, delightful, motivated life? People with excess intellectual work such as judges, prosecutors, lawyers, executives, doctors, psychologists, and teachers develop ATS more intensely. The most delicate and efficient people are often more stressed out. Below are some causes for ATS:

I.   Excess information
II.   Excess activities
III.   Excess intellectual work
IV.   Excessive worry
V.   Excessive demands
VI.   Excessive use of mobile phones
VII.   Excessive use of computers.

Excess information is the main cause for ATS. In the past, the amount of information doubled every two to three centuries. Today, it doubles every year.

We thought that this avalanche of information coming from TV, school, videogames, smartphones, newspapers, companies, was not such a significant problem, but today we know that the ARM phenomenon stores everything in the cerebral cortex without asking the Self's permission, thus saturating the Continuous Use Memory.

The CUM is the memory's conscious center. Metaphorically speaking, it represents a human being's circulation area inside a great city. At the most, this person daily visits up to 2% of the city's streets, avenues and stores. He sometimes visits peripheral areas, which is called Existential Memory or Unconscious Memory in the Multifocal Intelligence Theory, as I have already mentioned.

If we saturate the CUM by increasing this number to 5 or 10%, we will increase the levels of vital anxiety and overstimulate the autoflow phenomenon, which in turn will begin to read memory faster and uncontrollably, thus producing thoughts at a speed never seen before. This generates the Accelerated Thinking Syndrome.

I will once again use the metaphor of a city to explain these unconscious phenomena that act in milliseconds. We all have a circulation area in a city. In the city of São Paulo, a person visits one or two pharmacies. But there are hundreds of drugstores, and in distant neighborhoods too. If a person had to go to many different pharmacies to buy some medicine and took many different ways to get there, it might take a whole day or even a week. This could be bad for his health.

Similarly, when we overstretch the CUM, the circulation area of our "city of memory", we produce tiring and unproductive mental work. In many company environments, many people are well-informed and think a lot, but very superficially. Their original ideas disappear.

The MIT not only studies the process of construction of thoughts, but also the formation process of thinkers, among others. I am convinced that it is not the excess information and thoughts that determine the quality of ideas. Einstein had less information than most engineers and physicists have nowadays, and he went much further. It is not the amount, but the way we reorganize the data, which determines the degree of creativity.

Selecting information is crucial. But in this rushed society we are terrible at choosing our mind's menu. We gobble everything down without proper digestion. How are we not to become drastically stressed out? We are destroying the employees of our companies, choking up the teachers in our classrooms, causing the doctors in our hospitals to have heart attacks.

Let us then talk about the children of humanity. We adults can still endure the symptoms caused by ATS, but what about our children?

CHAPTER 11

Murdering Childhood

The social system has committed one of the most drastic collective murders: the murder of childhood. The world is shocked at the use of weapons of mass destruction, but keeps silent about the "weapons" in the social system that cause the mass destruction of our children's childhood.

Excess stimuli, activities, toys, ads, smartphones, videogames, TV, and school information saturate the CUM of the children of humanity, producing slaves of intellectual work and monitoring their thoughts at levels never seen before.

A seven-year-old child nowadays probably has more information than an emperor did in Ancient Rome, than Pythagoras, Socrates, Plato, Aristoteles or any of the great thinkers in Ancient Greece. So how to prevent children from being mentally agitated, distracted, impulsive, irritable, and with difficulty to develop their experiences? Impossible.

They are unstable, irritable, intolerant to setbacks, insecure in new situations, do not enjoy learning, and have a hard time discussing ideas in even low-stress situations.

We adults commit a crime by overstimulating the process of construction of thoughts. We do not realize that children need to learn to protect the emotion, filter stressful stimuli, develop pleasure through educational activities, and participate of creative processes that involve development, such as sports, music, painting, and contact with nature.

When some people see agitated and rebellious children and adolescents, they quickly blame the parents, saying that they were negligent and did not set boundaries or teach any values. Yes, some parents manifest such sickly behavior as educators, but most of them are just completely lost. They take action, but their words have no impact. They set limits, but their children constantly repeat the same mistakes. The cause is evident. Due to ATS, the younger generation no longer develops experiences that involve loss and frustration and, therefore, their ARM phenomenon does not store such experiences or form healthy centers of habitation of the Self, which are capable of enriching their personality traits. Their Self becomes rigid, disconnected, drifting, and most of the time self-sabotaging.

It has never been so hard to educate

Through my books, I have "shouted out" in many countries that we are violating the black box of the construction of thoughts of our children, which is very serious. We are sleeping, and at the same time, dreaming in fascination over the digital world we have created.

It has never been so hard to instruct a generation. No one is to blame. It is the system's fault. We all have our portion of responsibility in the murder of childhood. What hurts my soul is to know that these young people will become adults in an environment of global warming, food insecurity, and predatory competition, and will need a remarkable ability in leadership and creativity to give intelligent responses to these issues. However, it is unfortunate that we are not preparing them for the disturbed world that we ourselves created.

When children are affected by ATS in early childhood, up to age five, parents are ecstatic imagining that their children are geniuses. They do not notice the symptoms. They boast about how their children are smart, absorb information quickly, and have an answer for everything. To make things worse for these geniuses, their parents involve them in an ocean of activities (school, learning languages, music, sports), and also allow them to undiscriminatingly access social networks. This process agitates their mind even more.

These parents do not know that children need to have a childhood, to create, develop, stabilize their emotion, give depth to their feelings, put themselves in the place of others, and think before reacting. Otherwise, they will have an unstable, dissatisfied, irritable emotion that is intolerant to setbacks, and of course, thinks too much.

The years go by, and as the children become preteens and teens, parents begin to realize that something is wrong. The genius has disappeared. Their children need more and more to feel less and less. They are dissatisfied and undisciplined, have a hard time expressing gratitude, with self-esteem (how they feel) that is frail, are unable to accept "no" for an answer, impatient and demand everything immediately.

It is crucial that parents do not give excessive presents or clothes to their children or enroll them in multiple activities. It is just as crucial that parents win over their children's territory of emotion and know how to transfer their capital of experiences to them, that is, give them what money cannot buy. They should not let them connect to social networks and use smartphones all day long. The anxious use of these devices may cause psychological dependence, just like some drugs. Take their phone away from them for a day and see how they react. Moreover, children, as well as their parents, should never use these devices in excess at night or sleep next to them, for the screen emanates a blue light that affects the brain's metabolism, suppressing the production of sleep-inducing substances.

Parents that overprotect their children and give them everything they want provide fuel for ATS. As I comment in the book *Brilliant parents, fascinating teachers*, remember that good parents support their children and give them gifts, but brilliant parents go beyond: they give them their story and transfer their most excellent capital – their experiences. Many parents lose their kids because they are incapable of turning their relationship into a great adventure.

CHAPTER 12

Levels Of ATS

ATS: disarm it!

If there are many unused bricks at a construction site, should we consider them useful objects or waste? Excess information becomes waste and impairs boldness, the ability to observe, and assimilation. Executives that live with the paranoia of informing themselves without being selective crush their originality and creativity.

ATS encompasses professional stress (burnout syndrome) generated by the use of mobile phones, excess activities, information, work, and predatory competition. Apart from exceptional cases or very specific hours, a professional should prohibit himself from using his mobile phone on weekends. There will always be problems to solve and activities to perform.

In this competitive and high consumption society, we either learn to be human beings or become work machines. Many do not know what it is to be a simple human being walking the path of life in search of himself. He lives in beautiful houses, but never finds a home inside himself.

Do you have the ATS bomb lodged in your mind? If you do, you must disarm it. I repeat: those who think in excess without any management from the Self suffer of acute brain fatigue with serious consequences to their professional, emotional and social future.

We can accelerate everything in the outer world to our advantage: transportation, industrial automation, the speed of computer information, but we should never accelerate the construction of thoughts. The autoflow phenomenon, which should be man's greatest source of entertainment, motivation and inspiration, has become the greatest source of stress, anxiety and psychosomatic symptoms.

Degrees of seriousness of ATS

First level of ATS: always distracted

People affected with this first level are those who sit in front of us and seem to be listening, but suddenly begin to repeatedly move their fingers or impatiently tap their hands on their legs. For sure, these people are distracted and are not paying attention to what we are saying.

Distracted people are part of a large group. They look in a certain direction, but are completely disconnected. They read a text, but do not absorb anything. As we have seen, they have a disconnected, distracted Self.

Second level of ATS: does not enjoy the journey

These are the people who sit down to read a newspaper, magazine or book and always read it backwards. They are so mentally agitated that they do not have the patience to take the normal path.

Such people do not enjoy the process while working on their projects. They can hardly wait to conclude them. People with this level of ATS do not celebrate their victory even as they fight for success. They do not give themselves any rest. They only know how to "fight battles" and do not know how to live in times of peace.

Even though they are intelligent, they are incoherent within themselves. They do not enjoy their own success. Only their children or others close to them will enjoy it.

Third level of ATS: cultivates tedium

People affected with this level of ATS are so stressed that when someone invites them to a party, they leap for joy. They cannot wait to leave work and get ready. However, when they reach the party, problems soon begin to appear.

The speed of their thoughts is much greater than the pace of the party. They start to crack their knuckles, look around in every direction, and become restless. Five minutes later, they are so bored and stressed out that they burst out, "Let's leave!"

Those who suffer from this level of ATS are always looking for something that does not exist outside of themselves. Only inwardly. Such people abhor routine. They get tired of everything very quickly. They rarely relax or enjoy where they are. They usually think others are superficial and boring.

When they are at home with the remote control in their hand, they make everyone else crazy. They switch channels every minute. Their mind is so quick that they hate commercials.

Fourth level of ATS: cannot stand slow people

This group is represented by those who get tense and irritated just by being around slow people. They are impatient with those who do not "catch on" quickly, who do not have attitude, who take a long time to see problems and present solutions.

People with this level of ATS are incapable of teaching something two or three times since they lose their patience. They think their work colleagues have some kind of mental problem, low IQ or are careless, since they are unable to keep up with their rhythm or reasoning. They do not understand that it is not the people around them who are slow; they are the ones who are too quick. They are too efficient, proactive, determined, and enterprising. And keeping up with them is a huge challenge.

Professionals with this level of ATS want everyone else to be fast and stressed like themselves. They want everyone to experience the evil of the century. They are great for their companies, but I once again affirm: they are their own executioners. They most probably will be the wealthiest people in a cemetery or the best candidates for a hospital bed. Is it worth it?

Fifth level of ATS: plans vacation ten months in advance

This level of ATS represents the people who are so anxious and have such a high speed of thinking that they look at the calendar and start to plan vacation ten months in advance. The reason for this is that the previous vacation was not enough to make them feel rested. In some cases, it stressed them out even more.

People with this level of ATS are restless. They clock in day after day, month after month, anxiously waiting for that blessed vacation. Their mood improves one month before vacation. When the last day of work arrives, they say bye to their colleagues and say to themselves, "You stressed out people stay in the line of fire, I'm out of here!"

Everything seems perfect. This will be the best vacation of their lives, until they start to pack. Even while packing, they think they have excess baggage and stress out their children and partner.

These people get nervous with the terrible drivers they encounter on the way, instead of beginning to relax. They become impatient with traffic, accelerating and braking constantly. They do not look at the horizon or enjoy the scenery. They want to get to their destination quickly and put on some light clothes and flip-flops. Soon they will relax, they think.

On the first day of vacation, these people do not know why, but they are unable to relax. On the second day, they are so irritable that they act like a financial manager demanding everything from everyone. On the third day, their children and spouse cannot stand them anymore. On the fourth, not even they can stand themselves. On the fifth day, they are so affected by ATS that they want to return to the battlefield of work, because they only feel alive when in battle.

Sixth level of ATS: *turns retirement into a desert*

This level of ATS represents the people that anxiously dream of retirement. Month after month, year after year, they count how much time is left for them to leave the stressful environment of work. They like their colleagues, but cannot stand looking at them anymore. They get the shivers when they see their boss approaching. And if they themselves are the boss, they lose their sleep when thinking about having to demand results from their subordinates.

Everything irritates them. They do not enjoy work. They no longer love challenges. If they are teachers, the noise in the classroom is like a torture chamber. They dream about vacation as a breathless person gasps for oxygen. They dream about fishing, strolling around, sitting on the porch and reading books. After crossing the desert, they think that life will be an oasis.

After a very long wait, the great moment finally arrives: their well-deserved retirement. Friends celebrate. They themselves are in a great mood. The first week is wonderful: they visit friends, take care of their plants, read some books. However, as the weeks and months pass, ATS meets them head on. The dog starts to get on their nerves, friends are no longer fun, which makes them feel useless. They do not know how to talk about trivial things, only about work and living under pressure and demands.

Such people are not prepared to enjoy life, rest, or behold beauty. The outcome of over four decades of work is depression and psychosomatic disease. The oasis of retirement increased the temperature of their anxiety.

* * *

Of course, there are exceptions. Not everyone has these levels of ATS, but I am talking about a fact that affects millions of people to a greater or smaller degree. Those who are always at war at work and in their mind become addicted to battles. Never forget that the body retires, but the mind never does.

Due to high levels of ATS, people are very active nowadays. They are in full intellectual vigor at 60, 70 or 80 years of age. And they often have a vital need of feeling useful to society. They cannot retire without preparing a second journey of pleasure, leisure, dreams, philanthropic or remunerated work for themselves.

Otherwise, they will become ill and also make those around them ill.

CHAPTER 13

Serious Consequences Of ATS

The emotional, intellectual, social and physical consequences of ATS are huge. Some will probably astound us. They may not always be immediately apparent, but will surely manifest themselves in the future. I am going to highlight the emotional consequences.

Premature aging of the emotion: chronic dissatisfaction

Every time we hyper accelerate our thoughts, our emotion loses quality, stability and depth. There is a need for greater stimuli, applause, and recognition in order to gain a few crumbs of pleasure. Those who have high levels of ATS often cry out for more recognition, even while living constantly under the media's spotlight.

A hyper-accelerated mind results in the premature aging of the emotion, accompanied by a very characteristic state of discomfort: frequent complaints, irritability when confronted by setbacks, intolerance for those whose thinking or pace is different, lack of motivation, lack of concentration in pursuing one's dreams, difficulty enjoying one's successes. A person who is emotionally rich and young from the psychiatric point of view is capable of beholding beauty, enjoying life, singing in the morning, and turning little things into a feast for one's eyes.

Unfortunately, there are young people of 10, 12, 15 or 20 years of age who are emotionally older than many old people of 80 or 90 years of age. They have a rigid, self-sabotaging Self. They are experts at criticizing others, which represents the most evident symptom of an aged emotion. They want everything immediately. They have lost their vigor; they have no energy to take chances, create opportunities, or continue after a fall.

When such people look in the mirror, they start a battle with themselves, seeing only their defects and never their qualities. They are oppressed by the media's tyrannical standard of beauty. They do not know that beauty is in the eye of the beholder. They do not know how to praise their parents and teachers. They do not even know how to be thankful for life or value themselves. Their emotion swings between heaven and hell: at one moment happily soaring, but in the next moment, down in the dumps.

If so many young people are prematurely old in their emotion, how many adults are suffering from mental acceleration? Many are in an emotional asylum, paupers destitute of emotional resources. Some skillfully manage their business or profession, but are incapable of managing what I consider the most complex business of all: the human mind. They complain about everything and everyone. They relegate their quality of life to the bottom of the list.

Fortunately, the human emotion should and is able to rejuvenate itself. We can relax every day and learn to make the most out of little things. This is why some people who are biologically 80 years old have such unbelievable vigor. They love life. They enjoy getting out, traveling, taking risks, meeting people, discovering things and reinventing themselves. They have intuitively developed a managing Self that does not give in to the fear of death, pessimism, or suffering beforehand. For them, life is a pageant to be enjoyed, even while undergoing hardships.

Retardation of the emotion's maturity

We should never forget this mechanism: when people have considerable ATS and their Self is incapable of minimally managing thoughts, this jeopardizes the process of handling loss, deception, defeat, and boundaries. The ARM phenomenon does not build healthy centers of light windows in the cerebral cortex, which will support the complex functions of intelligence such as proactivity, self-determination, resilience, and tolerance.

The consequence? Not only the premature aging of the emotion, which I just mentioned, but also the slowing down of maturity. Can you imagine an adult with an aged emotion who is at the same time immature?

Do you know executives, doctors, psychologists, lawyers, journalists, or politicians that cannot be contradicted, criticized or confronted? They are examples of people who are emotionally old and intellectually immature. They are chronically dissatisfied and discouraged, complain about everything – therefore, they are old – and present authoritarian behavior. They cannot accept being challenged and they never recognize their errors or apologize.

Egocentrism, selfishness and individualism are not and have never been signs of power: they are symptoms of a prematurely aged psyche which is also childish. In terms of maturity, every dictator acts like a child.

Emotional immaturity manifests the neurotic need for power, for always being right, for controlling others, and is accompanied by the inability to deal with boundaries, to wait for results, to accept not being the center of attention.

I honestly do not know anyone who is fully mature, whether in the field of philosophy, spirituality, medicine or psychology. If we map ourselves out thoroughly, we will find some kind of immaturity. We all need to review our story. Some people are fascinating when not in stressful situations, but become unrecognizable when put under pressure.

A mature and empathizing Self (who knows how to put itself in the place of others) finds pleasure in being altruistic and promoting others, knows how to boost its self-esteem, and does not ignorantly sell its well-being. In other words, it knows how to protect itself.

Due to ATS, children and adolescents are collectively losing their ingenuity, creativity, and ability to overcome conflicts and adapt to adversities. They do not know how to accept "no" for an answer, how to weep or overcome hardships, how to deal with a breakup with a boyfriend or girlfriend. Patience is a rare article. They need extensive and elaborate stimuli, like an expensive dish ordered from a fancy menu instead of a hamburger.

Those who do not fight for their dreams and want everything immediately will forever be children. This is why many 40-year-old professionals have the emotional maturity of an 18-year-old and many 18-year-olds have the emotional age of a 10year-old.

Reprocessing the Accelerated Thinking Syndrome in order to nourish emotional maturity is crucial for having a free and accomplished mind. Otherwise, the word "happiness" will only exist in the dictionary, but will never be written in our story.

Premature death of emotional life

Emotional time is not the same as physical time. One of the most serious consequences of ATS is the premature death of the emotion, or perhaps better put, of the perception of time. I will give an example to explain this phenomenon. Do we live longer than the people in the Middle Ages? The answer is obvious. Biologically, we live twice as long. At that time, the average life expectancy was 40 years. Tonsillitis could develop into a serious infection, since there were no antibiotics. Hollywood presents a distorted picture of the glamour of women of the noble class. In reality, many princesses had already lost their teeth by the age of 20 and had to keep their lips always pursed.

Today we live on the average from 70 to 80 years and this is on the rise. But let me ask you something else: from the emotional point of view, do we live more or less than the Greeks, the Romans, or those from medieval times?

The Accelerated Thinking Syndrome causes us to live a faster life in our mind, which distorts our perception of time. We live longer biologically, but die earlier emotionally. Eighty years go by faster than twenty years did in the past. Medicine has prolonged physical life and the social environment has decreased emotional time.

Does it not feel like we fell asleep and suddenly woke up with our current age? Does it not seem like our life has gone by so very quickly? We are so busy with mental and professional activities, that we do not have time to enjoy, taste and assimilate the food of daily experiences. As I said, we are in the emotional fast-food age, in which we gulp down our nourishment. We do not know how to take time to love, to listen to, to converse, to dream, to absorb or even to chat.

Do you feel as if the months and years are flying by? This is serious. One of our greatest challenges is to expand our time. But who has a Self that is trained to increase the perception of time? We have no idea what to do with tedium. Children are so accelerated that when they sit still for five minutes they complain, "There's nothing to do in this house!" We are addicted to activity, information, mobile phones. We are addicted to asphyxiating time and addicted to thinking.

We should live out our experiences slowly and gently, like when we savor an ice cream cone on a hot summer day. Our Self should turn a day into a week, a week into a month, a month into a year. Anxious, impatient, restless people who hate routine and want everything immediately will not enjoy life as it passes by. They are their emotion's worst enemy. What about me? What about you?

Emotional defenselessness and the development of psychiatric disorders

Another consequence of ATS is emotional defenselessness. Restless people who thinks too much do not develop the ability to filter stressful stimuli. They very easily build killer windows. Their emotion is a desolate land without an owner. Any slander, criticism or injustice defeats it. Loss and deception affect it to the point of turning their day, week, month, and even life into a desert. The autoflow phenomenon controls their emotion, reading and re-reading these experiences, thus turning their mind into hell.

People without emotional protection run the risk of developing hypersensitivity. Not only do they worry about other people's pain, but also experience such pain; not only do they think about tomorrow, but suffer with the future. In addition, they are overly concerned about their image and what others think of them, especially in this day of online social networks. As a result of all this, they experience increased ATS and set themselves up for depression, panic syndrome or psychosomatic illnesses.

I have already treated celebrities and multimillionaires concerned with their physical integrity. They had bulletproof cars and bodyguards, but had not learned how to protect their emotion. They had not acquired insurance against stressful stimuli caused by others or by their own mind. They did not know how to reprocess their self-punishing thoughts, excessive self-demands, and asphyxiating worries. Although they lived as kings, they were begging for peace and joy.

Many people will not tolerate trash in their car, kitchen, office or room, but allow trash to accumulate in the most fascinating room of all: their own mind. Is this not a paradox? How can we avoid becoming victims of anxiety if we are negligent in the only environment in which it is inadmissible for us not to take action?

Most people lock up their houses, even in the world's safest countries. But their personality is an unprotected house. An unprotected emotion has a drifting Self. Happy moments alternate with sad ones, a feeling of well-being alternates with isolation, and security and jealousy are part of the same menu.

Always remember that our worse enemies are not outside of us. It is vital to develop abilities for managing thoughts in this stressful society, otherwise our emotion will be a helmless boat, a driverless car. It would be practically impossible to avoid an accident. And it is impossible not to be in this vehicle, for we ourselves are the vehicle.

Other consequences of ATS

Besides all the emotional consequences caused by the Accelerated Thinking Syndrome, there are other equally important ones, which I will briefly mention.

Psychosomatic diseases

Chronic (long-lasting) anxiety can cause many psychosomatic symptoms, hypertension, tachycardia, "lump in the throat", hair loss and auto-immune illnesses. It can also trigger, accelerate or influence the development of certain kinds of heart attacks and cancer.

Endangerment of creativity

A person with a hyper-accelerated mind has a harder time opening memory windows and coming up with brilliant answers for stressful situations. Thinking in excess blocks inventiveness as well as the imagination.

Endangerment of overall intellectual performance

In the long run, ATS jeopardizes the process of observing, assimilating, rescuing and organizing data. Oral and written exams can be adversely affected by a mind that thinks excessively and is overly occupied with its intellectual performance and the opinion of teachers and parents. Chronic (permanent) stress caused by ATS can hinder memory windows from opening.

Deterioration of social relations

A hyper-accelerated mind tends to be impulsive, does not think before reacting, and has little patience with others, be they children, friends, spouse or work colleagues. This behavior jeopardizes the affection, stability and deepness of interpersonal relationships. Many couples begin their relationship in the heaven of affection and end up in the hell of irritability.

Difficulty in cooperating with others in a group

An agitated mind has a harder time expressing its thoughts, discussing ideas, accepting others, being friendly (pleasant) or empathetic (being able to see through others' eyes). As we have seen, a hyper-accelerated person pressures everyone around them to keep up with their frenetic pace, which is practically an impossibility for "simple mortals". ATS endangers the mental health of a human being, the future of a company, the GNP (Gross National Product) of a country, and the sustainability of the environment and of the human species.

CHAPTER 14

How To Manage the Accelerated Thinking Syndrome – Part I

I am going to broach eight very important techniques for combating the evil of the century: anxiety resulting from the Accelerated Thinking Syndrome. It is not easy to fully cure this problem in this stressful, fast-paced, restless society. But if it is not possible to eliminate it, we should at least manage it. Our emotional, social and professional future is intimately linked to whether we succeed at this task or not. I will divide these techniques into two parts.

1. Enabling the Self to be the author of its own story

All over the world, fitness centers help people exercise their bodies, schools develop scholastic and technical abilities, and driving courses teach people to drive automobiles. There are, however, practically no schools that teach and train the Self to drive the most complex vehicle of all, the human mind.

Enabling the Self to be a mental manager is not only crucial for decelerating thoughts, but also fundamental for fostering a healthy emotion and a creative mind. Yet such qualification seems unattainable in this superficial society. However, it is possible! Is your Self qualified? Because we have such a rich sensorial system that connects us to the outer world, we are addicted to using it instead of equipping ourselves to intervene in the mental terrain. Once we have already sickened, we assign responsibility to clinical psychiatry and psychotherapy, or to spirituality, philosophy and self-help authors. We make serious errors by not developing psychiatric, psychological, educational and sociological tools for preventing emotional disorders and strengthening the most important functions of intelligence.

When a new virus appears, the World Health Organization (WHO) and scientists from innumerous universities spring into action to avoid an epidemic. However, we do not despair with the lack of technology for preventing phobias, depression, anorexia, panic, bullying, and the evil of the century, ATS. These symptoms affect billions of people in modern societies. Yet we seem to be in hibernation.

The WHO, scientists, and university professors should be mobilized to the vital need of managing thoughts, protecting the emotion, filtering stressful stimuli, seeing things through others' eyes, thinking of humanity as a whole. Our species is going through a crisis, not due only to terrorist attacks, drug epidemics, urban violence, school violence, violence against women, consumerism, pedophilia, and discrimination, but also because the hyper construction of thoughts is attacking the mind and the ability of the Self as manager of our psyche.

You should choose if you will just sit in the audience, passively watching the thoughts produced by unconscious phenomenon (memory trigger, memory windows, and especially the autoflow) or if you will take over as the script director of your story. Depending on your decision, the techniques which I will now mention can be vital.

We will never have complete control over our fate, as dreamt of by Jean-Paul Sartre and other existentialists. We will never be completely autonomous as yearned for by Paulo Freire. But our hands are not tied. We can and should stop being mere supporting actors and take up our role as the leading actor in the mental theater.

If our Self is equipped to know the last boundary of science, the process of construction of thoughts, and taught to manage our intellect, a majority of our prisons will become museums, many policemen will become poets, many psychiatrists and psychologists will have time to plant flowers. What about wars? They will no longer hinge on weapons of bloodshed, but on ideas which inject love, altruism and tolerance into the world. We will no longer think in fiefdoms, but as one human family.

2. Free to think, but not a slave to thoughts

To be free to think is very different from being enslaved by thoughts. To be free in our mind is to give flight to imagination, to be free to innovate, to take risks, and to propose new ideas. It is to fascinate our students, influence our children, and surprise those with whom we choose to share our story. It is to speak words that have never before been spoken and to manifest pleasantly unexpected behaviors. For instance, it is to say "Thank you for existing!" to those whom we love; or "Although you have upset me, I wish you success!" to those who let us down.

On the other hand, to be a slave to ATS is to have no defense against pessimism, conformism, self-pity, self-abandonment, self-punishment, feelings of guilt, and mental agitation. It is to be choking inwardly and to be without responsive action. It is to be terrorized in our own mind and to keep silent. In order to free ourselves from these prisons, we need to develop non-genetic abilities.

My books are used in institutes for geniuses to help them develop abilities that they lack and make them productive. But I am sure that we can all develop abilities that surpass those provided by our genes. When a human being learns to put himself in the place of others, and to propose instead of impose his ideas, he becomes a genius in empathy. When he learns to have resilience, he becomes a genius in his capability to deal with loss. When he decides to be free and transforms chaos into an opportunity for growth, he becomes a genius in innovation and creativity.

3. Managing suffering in advance

One of the most important tasks of the Self is to daily manage thoughts that weaken and block intelligence, especially those that imprint stress caused by anticipating the future. However, it is surprising how our Self prepares for its own funeral before the proper time.

Many of us criticize mysticism but act like second-rate fortunetellers. We suffer with the predictions of our mind. Over 90% of our worries concerning the future will never come true. And the other 10% will happen differently from what we imagine. It is not possible to have a stable and healthy emotion without confronting such daily worries with a shock of reality. The Self can and should challenge and refute low-quality thoughts. Not to do so is to be naïve and not recognize that the ARM phenomenon is imprinting such thoughts.

Nothing fuels the evil of the century – anxiety caused by ATS – as much as suffering with what has not yet happened. Our Self should think about the future only to dream and develop strategies for overcoming challenges and difficulties. It is unfortunate that so many allow themselves to be haunted by the future. They sabotage their quality of life in the present.

4. Performing mental hygiene through the DCD technique

To perform mental hygiene is as important as or even more important than personal hygiene. If we do not learn how to perform it, we cannot alleviate the Accelerated Thinking Syndrome, and even less re-edit killer or traumatic windows.

An excellent tool for performing efficient mental hygiene, which we have highly recommended in over sixty countries, is the DCD technique (doubt, criticize and determine).

Why is doubting so crucial? Because it is the beginning of wisdom in philosophy. No one frees creativity, breaks out of the mold and produces important ideas if he has not learned to manipulate the art of doubting, even if intuitively. Everything we believe in controls us. If what we believe in is sickly, this can keep us ill for all our life. To be able to doubt being controlled by fear, insecurity, anxiety, impulsiveness, irritability, and low self-esteem is the basic foundation for overcoming them.

And why is criticizing so vital? Because criticism and self-criticism are the foundation of wisdom in psychology. Criticizing each disturbing thought and anguishing emotion, as well as the Self's passivity, is to nurture clear thinking and mental maturity. Many are great at criticizing others and do not forgive failures to the point of being insufferable, but lack the capability to criticize themselves. In their own eyes, they are candidates to be gods, since with their rigid Self, they never question their inflexibility, agitated mind or morbid thoughts.

To complete the technique, we should always use strategic determination. This tool is the beginning of wisdom in the human resources field. Determination is the source of discipline, self-determination, and the ability to fight for one's goals. Without discipline, our goals become superficial motivations, not life projects. Without self-determination, our projects dissipate in the heat of hardships.

The DCD technique does not replace psychological treatment, for it is an educational technique. Yet it makes mental hygiene effective. How often do we take a shower? In the twenty thousand sessions of psychotherapy and psychiatric consultations that I have given, I have seen astounding illnesses. I had a patient who took a shower forty times a day. After her shower, two unconscious phenomena that build thoughts in milliseconds came into action: the memory trigger and the killer window. While she dried herself, the trigger opened the killer window that told her that the towel was dirty. This closed the memory circuit, and the Self, choked down with anxiety, repeated the bath ritual.

On an average, we take a shower every twenty hours and brush our teeth every four to six hours. Let us then recall: what about mental hygiene? How long does it take us to perform it? Let us not forget – at the most, five seconds. When we produce a distressing emotion or thought, we should carry out the DCD technique in the silence of our mind, while the window is open and the ARM phenomena is at work. Otherwise, whatever is registered can no longer be deleted, only re-edited.

Yet it is amazing how we are slow and timid in our mind. No wonder we get ill so easily. We should turn the table against everything that steals away our peace. It is like frequently giving silent shouts of liberty. How? What words should we use? There are no rules. We should apply the DCD technique daily and freely, using our own culture and ability.

Countless people from many countries have improved their quality of life, relieved their anxiety and rescued the leadership of the Self by using this psychological and preventive education technique. I have received many messages from people, who because they use this technique daily, have been able to reprocess and even overcome their ideas of suicide, and are no longer enslaved by their emotion. DCD has also been used to complement psychiatric and psychotherapeutic treatment.

To doubt everything that imprisons us, to criticize each thought that hurts us, and to determine a strategy for where we want to arrive with our quality of life and social relations are crucial tasks for the Self. Remember that doubting and criticizing come before determining. Otherwise, DCD will be an unsustainable self-help technique instead of a scientific and effective technique.

CHAPTER 15

How To Manage the Accelerated Thinking Syndrome – Part II

5. Reprocessing false beliefs

False beliefs are more powerful than occasional distressing thoughts and emotions. The latter can be built from small platforms of tensional windows, while the former are killer centers of habitation of the Self, and therefore establish enormous dungeons.

Some examples of false beliefs are the feelings of incapability, inferiority complex, shyness, conformism, the neurotic need to be perfect (demanding too much of oneself), the conviction that one is programmed to be depressed, social phobia, dependence, anxiety. Some people are generous toward others, but hard on themselves. They are always punishing themselves, for they have the anxious need to be the best professional, friend or parent. Others believe that they will be shy for the rest of their lives, that they will always have a hard time speaking in public and discussing ideas. There are others who think they are condemned to being depressive or will have to deal with their claustrophobia forever.

Many of these people are wonderful, intelligent, generous human beings, but not to themselves. They often live in dungeons of their own building. As we have studied, thoughts can be virtual and turn the truth into something unattainable, but false beliefs have the power to transform unreality into an absolute truth, thus creating mental prisons for the Self that can last throughout life. Because such beliefs build mental prisons, they further ATS.

The self-sabotaging Self of such people is always building traps for them to be kept in constant misery, even though others may greatly admire them. It is vital to daily apply the DCD technique to false beliefs in order to re-edit the sickly centers inhabited by the Self.

Another powerful technique is the roundtable of the Self. In this technique, the Self meets daily with our false beliefs in the silence of our mind. In this meeting, it establishes a firm self-dialogue, or even better, an open, sincere, honest discussion with the unfounded lies, distorted concepts and standards created by false beliefs.

We should apply the DCD technique when at a distance from stressful situations, when the "monster" is hibernating, that is, when the killer center is not open. The DCD technique re-edits killer windows, and the technique of the roundtable of the Self builds parallel light windows around the traumatic center.

These two powerful techniques are for those who want to exit the audience, step onto the stage of their own mind, and take on the important roles of managing thoughts, protecting the emotion and filtering stressful stimuli.

6. Stop being a work machine: the most efficient patient in the hospital

The sixth tool for alleviating the Accelerated Thinking Syndrome meets the need of people who are extremely successful in their profession. As I mentioned, the best professionals never stop. They are addicted to work, performing activities, building, inventing. To be enterprising is vital to become a project builder, but to be overly enterprising is the best way to destroy one's own emotional health. Although they are unconscious about it, it seems like these professionals want to be the wealthiest occupants of the cemetery…

They clearly know that they are mortal, but live as if they were eternal, or as if they were to live for thousands of years. There is no doubt that in some moments of our professional story we have to sacrifice ourselves, seize the opportunities, and work a lot, including on weekends and holidays. However, this sacrifice should be temporary and only for some months or, at the most, a few years.

No one is invulnerable. Some overwork themselves for decades, not to earn money, but to fulfill the needs of others and to enrich their meaning of life. Some religious people and philanthropists dedicate themselves to the needs of others, which is noble. But while they may be happy helping others, there is a high "price" to pay, for if altruism is not well managed, its demands become wearing. It is not possible to give excessively of oneself without depleting mental health.

Even a brilliant mind like that of the Master of masters suffered unprecedented emotional fatigue on his last night, two thousand years ago. A psychological and nontheological analysis of his behavior shows that he anticipated the suffering that was to come the next day, preparing himself to bear the unbearable. Therefore, he hyper accelerated his thoughts and had hematidrosis (blood sweat), a rare symptom produced by great stress. He almost had a heart attack before dying on the cross, having received the Roman sentence. But he did not bow before his anxiety. He protected his emotion, managed his thoughts and turned chaos into poetry. Hundreds of millions of people who regard him in different religions probably have not studied the mental mechanisms that he used when going through these stressful situations. Too many wallow in the mud of anxiety.

The use of such mechanisms explain Jesus' phenomenal lucidity in trying to rescue his most educated student at the exact moment when he was betraying his master. Jesus had the courage to call Judas a friend and ask him a question, which as we have seen, is the beginning of wisdom in philosophy.

"Friend, why have you come?" This indicates that he was not afraid of being betrayed, but of losing a friend. Who was this master who invested everything he had in those who let him down? Unfortunately, Judas entered a double P killer window, which generated intense guilt, closed the memory circuit and hijacked his Self in the only place where he should never have sold his freedom. Judas had social vocation, he wanted to help others, but when he needed to protect himself, he failed, becoming his own executioner.

Many scientists spend their entire life researching day and night to produce knowledge, including vaccines to ease the suffering of others. They have an uncontrollable motivation to contribute to humanity. However, they do not manage their stress or protect themselves. They close themselves up in their own world and many of them become ill.

With all humility, in order to produce the Freemind – a free, worldwide program launched in the United States for master's students, doctoral students, and leaders from over thirty countries, which has twelve tools that contribute to the development of a free mind and a healthy emotion, – I had to work on many weekends and forgo many hours of rest, including year-end holidays. But I was aware that it was something temporary and that it was for a good cause.

There are many essential classes of professionals that contribute to the sustainability of the functioning of society, and that have an inhumane workload. I would like to highlight two of these: judges (magistrates) and public prosecutors. It is amazing how the federal and state governments of a country do not consider the quality of life of these honorable professionals. Judges seem to do the impossible in a conflicting society that, due to ATS and mind traps, have little capability of protecting the emotion and solving conflicts pacifically, thus preferring to take the path of legal proceedings. There are over a hundred million legal procedures in Brazil against an inexpressive number of less than twenty thousand judges. Countless magistrates, because they are altruistic, destroy their physical and emotional health working at night, sacrificing their families, weekends and even holidays.

Moreover, many of them suffer external threats. But the first and worst enemy is the one that comes from inside, resulting from the crushing weight of an overload of intellectual work, which destroys the quality of life. The Accelerated Thinking Syndrome leads these professionals to feel tired when they wake up, have headaches, muscle pains, anxiety, suffering in advance, sleep deficit, memory deficit. How can we be a just and fraternal society if we unjustly treat the very ones who are responsible for carrying out justice? We need to give more attention to all professionals from the legal system.

Being concerned with the well-being of others is a good way to minimize the ghosts we create. It is our privilege and obligation to involve ourselves in society, since we have received for free what is essential for survival: the air, our heartbeat, the glucose cycle of over three million cells that make up our body. However, those who are concerned with the pain of others have to manage their thoughts more efficiently, for as I said, we will always pay a high psychosomatic price for altruism. And one of the mechanisms that can most relieve ATS and protect ourselves is to decrease the expectation of receiving something in return. No one can frustrate us more than those to whom we dedicate ourselves.

From the strictly professional angle, the problem is that many very efficient and responsible people are irresponsible with their emotional health. They never switch themselves off. They do not take pleasure in their success. The greater their financial success, the more they want to work. When they reach the victory stand, their joy lasts a short amount of time, for they soon begin another journey. If they sit on a porch to behold beauty for one or two hours, they feel bored. They can never slow down.

I am writing the last words of this book in the Czech Republic, a country where my books are published. In Prague, the cultural and architectural richness is impressive. But I notice that Japanese, Chinese, Germans and Americans with an executive air look tense, are always in a rush, and never slow down. They want to visit as many places possible and take quick pictures, but do not slow down enough to carefully observe the story, tears, nightmares and dreams behind the monuments. Many do not even seem to be on vacation, but merely consume touristic products. They land up even more tired than when they began. In order for vacation to really be a "vacation", they should clear their mind, calm down their emotion, and swallow high doses of pleasure, sleep, energy and rest.

7. Not being an information machine

In these days, any computer, no matter how slow, has the capacity of "storing" and recovering more information than the most ingenious brain. But data quantity is not what gives relevance to creativity and intellectual efficiency.

My theory does not only encompass the formation of the Self, but also the formation process of brilliant minds. I am convinced that boldness, self-criticism, resilience, self-confidence, self-esteem, imagination, multifocal reasoning, logical reasoning, and the capacity to open the maximum number of windows in stressful situations are more important for the production of new solutions, innovation, and brilliant answers than a super memory saturated with data.

Computers are structured to have an excellent program and a super database. Thinkers are produced by a good database and high doses of the most complex functions of intelligence.

Those who do not select books, texts, techniques, courses, and articles, run two great risks: worsening the Accelerated Thinking Syndrome and blocking creativity. Remember that Einstein, Freud, and so many other producers of knowledge had less data in their memory than most of their disciples from the following generations. So how did they go so far?

They reprocessed their false beliefs and feeling of incapability, intuitively used the DCD technique (they questioned, criticized and determined), and additionally, were bold, intuitive, lost their sleep for innumerable nights, were mocked, excluded, and discredited. But whoever wins without facing crises and accidents wins without glory...

8. Not being a traitor to the quality of life

The eighth and last tool for decreasing ATS is related to a dramatic error. Before talking about it, allow me to ask you: have you ever been betrayed in some way? Many of us have already been betrayed. Only friends betray us: enemies disappoint us. Only the people to whom we dedicate ourselves are able to hurt us so badly.

What about you? Have you ever betrayed someone? Maybe we are embarrassed to answer. If we are honest, we know we all have been there! And what is worse, we betray that which is most relevant for having a free mind and a healthy emotion. We betray our sleep, our weekends, our vacation, our relaxation. We betray the precious time we could have to ourselves, performing mental hygiene, reprocessing our false beliefs, nourishing ourselves with the pleasure of living. We are all traitors.

And our betrayal does not stop here. We betray the dialogue with the people who are dearest to us. We betray the time we should spend with our children, friends, spouse or partner. Dialogue is the best way to transfer our most notable legacy, our new experiences. And transferring this legacy is crucial, not only to alleviate ATS, but to also ground relationships and give flavor to life.

Despite having treated many patients and having met many people, I have not lost pleasure in maintaining dialogue. Each human being, regardless social status, cultural background or fragmented emotion, is a world to be discovered, a universe to be explored. I think it strange that people do not look at each other in an elevator, but at the floor number. We all have the need for dialogue. Yet we hide ourselves so easily.

Since I am a critic of celebrity worshipping, I rarely give interviews in Brazil, although I do so in other countries. I have millions of readers, but people seldom recognize me. Once, something unexpected happened. Whenever I travel by plane, I make an effort to meet whoever is next to me. It is an opportunity for dialogue, to find out more about an incredible human being. I sat next to a thirty-five-year-old man. He was impatient, anxious, constantly fidgeting with his fingers and hands. He probably wanted the plane to fly at light speed.

I soon asked him, "Is everything okay?" He did not want to talk. He roughly answered, "Yes." I then asked, "What do you do?" He gruffly answered, "I'm an executive." *What kind of executive?* I thought to myself. Drug trafficking, food, clothes? It was most obvious that the man did not want to be bothered by a stranger. And to shut me up, he pulled out a book from his case. What book? *The Dreamseller*!

I looked up at him and said, "I know the author of that book, and it will soon be made into a movie." The man thought I was mocking him. Doubting me, he laconically affirmed, "He lives abroad!"

Then I asked him to open the book on a certain page, where "this and that" would be written. He suspiciously checked what I was saying and was impressed with the fact that I knew the text. He frowned and with an authoritarian tone asked, "How do you know that?" So I presented myself as the author of book.

The man continued to believe that I was making fun of him. He raised his voice and demanded, "Show me your passport!". We were on a domestic flight and I did not have my passport with me, neither did I need to prove anything to him. I answered, "I'm sorry for the joke. I'm not the author."

At that moment, the flight attendant, who knew me, showed up and said, "Dr. Cury, I'm reading one of your books." The executive was finally convinced that I was the author. He suddenly hugged me, pulled out his phone and said, "We're going on Facebook!"

Was all that necessary? I just wanted to start a dialogue with another human being. But unfortunately, as I have observed before, we are dying younger emotionally, in spite of living longer biologically. We do not know how to manage our emotion, expand time, hold dialogues, talk about ourselves, spend time on things that money cannot buy.

I wish you success on this fascinating journey.

Paying our "debts" and correcting routes

We should remember that one of the most serious consequences of ATS is the premature death of emotional time. We lead such an agitated and busy existence that when we stop to think about life, we get scared. Like I mentioned previously, it seems like we have fallen asleep and did not see time go by. We miss out on the best of ourselves, our children, friends, and spouse just by wallowing in the mud of worries, entrenched in our mental battles. The consequence is that many notable human beings are on the verge of physical and emotional failure.

Those who are not attentive to their quality of life have an unpayable debt to themselves. What is the size of your debt to your quality of life? You will only know if you map out your mind in a transparent and honest manner.

To manage the anxiety produced by the evil of the century, ATS, and pay off our "debts", we should use these techniques daily. To have the courage to journey into ourselves, acknowledge our weaknesses, admit our insanities, make corrections to our routes, and educate ourselves to be the authors of our own story is, above all, to have a love story with life.

No one who can do this for you, not your children, partner, friends, neurologist, psychiatrist, psychologist or books. Only you yourself... Do not betray the best thing you possess!

The End (or the beginning)!

Bibliographical References

ADLER, Alfred. *Understanding Human Nature*. Garden City, NY: Garden City Publishing Co., 1927.

ADORNO, Theodor W. *Educação e emancipação*. [Education and Emancipation]. Rio de Janeiro: Paz e Terra, 1971.

CHAUÍ, Marilena. *Convite à filosofia*. [Invitation to Philosophy]. São Paulo: Ática, 2000.

COSTA, Newton C.A. *Ensaios sobre os fundamentos da lógica*. [Essays on the Foundations of Logic]. São Paulo: Edusp, 1975.

CURY, Augusto. *Armadilhas da mente*. [Mind Traps]. Rio de Janeiro: Arqueiro, 2013.

_____. *A fascinante construção do Eu*. [The Fascinating Construction of the Self]. São Paulo: Academia da Inteligência, 2011.

_____. *Em busca do sentido da vida*. [In search of the meaning of life]. São Paulo: Planeta do Brasil, 2013.

_____. *Inteligência multifocal*. [Multifocal Intelligence]. São Paulo: Cultrix, 1999.

_____. *O colecionador de lágrimas*. [The Tear Collector]. São Paulo: Planeta do Brasil, 2012.

_____. *O código da inteligência*. [The Intelligence Code]. Rio de Janeiro: Ediouro, 2009.

_____. *O mestre dos mestres.* [The Master of Masters]. São Paulo: Academia de Inteligência, 2000.

_____. *Pais brilhantes, professores fascinantes.* [Brilliant Parents, Fascinating Teachers]. Rio de Janeiro: Sextante, 2003.

DESCARTES, René. *O discurso do método.* [Discourse on the Method]. Brasília: UnB, 1981.

DUARTE, André. Duarte, A. "A dimensão política da filosofia kantiana segundo Hannah Arendt". [The Political Dimension of Kant's Philosophy According to Hannah Arendt]. In: Arendt, H. *Lições sobre a filosofia política de Kant.* Rio de Janeiro: Relume Dumará, 1993.

FEUERSTEIN, Reuven. *Instrumental Enrichment — An Intervention Program for Cognitive Modificability.* Baltimore: University Park Press, 1980.

FOUCAULT, Michel. *A doença e a existência.* [Mental Illness and Existence]. Rio de Janeiro: Folha Carioca, 1998.

FRANKL, Viktor Emil. *A questão do sentido em psicoterapia.* [The Question of Meaning in Psychotherapy]. Campinas: Papirus, 1990.

FREIRE, Paulo. *Pedagogia dos sonhos possíveis.* [Pedagogy of Possible Dreams]. São Paulo: Unesp, 2005.

FREUD, Sigmund. *Obras completas.* [The Complete Works]. Madrid:

Editorial Biblioteca Nueva, 1972.

FROMM, Erich. *Análise do homem.* [Man for himself]. Rio de Janeiro: Zahar, 1960.

GARDNER, Howard. *Multiple intelligences: The theory in practice.* New York: Basic Books, 1993.

GOLEMAN, Daniel. *Inteligência emocional.* [Emotional Intelligence]. Rio de Janeiro: Objetiva, 1995.

HALL, Lindzey. Theories of Personality. New York: Wiley, 1957.

HEIDEGGER, Martin. *Os Pensadores.* São Paulo: Abril Cultural, 1989.

HUSSERL, Edmund. *La Filosofía como Ciencia Estricta.* [Philosophy as a Rigorous Science]. Buenos Aires: Nova, 1980.

JUNG, Carl Gustav. *O desenvolvimento da personalidade.* [The Development of Personality]. Petrópolis: Vozes, 1961.

KAPLAN, Harold I.; SADOCH, Benjamin J.; GREBB, Jack A. Kaplan and Sadock's Synopsis of Psychiatry. Behavioural Sciences/Clinical Psychiatry. 7th edition. Williams & Wilkins: Baltimore, 1994.

KIERKEGAARD, Sören Aabye. *Diário de um sedutor e outras obras.* [The Seducer's Diary and other works]. São Paulo: Abril Cultural, 1989. LIPMAN, Matthew. *O pensar na educação.* [Thinking in Education]. Petrópolis:Vozes, 1995.

MASTEN, Ann S. *Ordinary Magic: Resilience Processes in Development.* American Psychologist, 56(3), 2001.

_____; GARMEZY, Norman Risk. "Vulnerability and Protective Factors in Developmental Psychopathology". In: LAHEY. Benjamin B.; KAZDIN, Alan E (eds.). *Advances in clinical child psychology: 8.* New York: Plenum Press, 1985.

MORIN, Edgar. *O homem e a morte*. [Man and Death]. Rio de Janeiro: Imago, 1997.

_____. *Seven Complex Lessons in Education for the Future*. Paris: UNESCO, 1999.

MUCHAIL, Salma T. "Heidegger e os Pré-Socráticos". [Heidegger and the Pre-Socratics]. In: MARTINS, Joel; Dichtchekenian, Maria Fernanda S.F. Beirão (orgs.). *Temas fundamentais de fenomenologia*. São Paulo: Moraes, 1984.

NACHMANOVITCH, Stephen. *Free Play: Improvisation in Life and Art*. Los Angeles: J.P. Tarcher, 1990.

PIAGET, Jean. *Biologia e conhecimento*. [Biology and Knowledge]. Petrópolis: Vozes, 1996.

PINKER, S. *How the Mind Works*. New York: W. W. Norton & Company, 1997.

SARTRE, Jean-Paul. *O ser e o nada*. [Being and Nothingness]. Petrópolis: Vozes, 1997.

STEINER, Claude. *Educação emocional*. [Achieving Emotional Literacy]. Rio de Janeiro: Objetiva: 1997.

STERNBERG, Robert J. Beyond IQ: A triarchic theory of human intelligence. New York: Cambridge University Press, 1985.

YUNES, Maria Angela M. *A questão triplamente controvertida da resiliência em famílias de baixa renda*. [The triply controversial issue of resilience in low income families]. Doctorate thesis, Pontifícia Universidade Católica de São Paulo: São Paulo, 2001.

YUNES, Maria Angela M.; SZYMANSKI, Heloísa. "Resiliência: noção, conceitos afins e considerações críticas". [Resilience: idea, similar concepts and critical considerations]. In: TAVARES, José. (Org.) *Resiliência e educação*. São Paulo: Cortez, 2001.

The Intelligence School

Imagine a school that not only teaches language to children and adolescents, but also the discussion of ideas, the ability to put oneself in the place of others, and to think before reacting in order to develop healthy relationships. A school that not only teaches numerical math but the mathematics of the emotion, in which dividing produces an increase, and that teaches resilience: the ability to deal with loss and frustration. Continue to imagine a school that teaches its students to manage thoughts and protect their emotion for the prevention of mental disorders. Even more, think about a school whose educational goal is to produce creative, bold, altruistic and tolerant thinkers instead of repeaters of information.

It seems uncommon for a school to teach these more complex functions of intelligence in the theater of the nations, but now there is a program called Intelligence School (E.I.), which can be added to the school curriculum once a week. It offers rich didactic material to help your child's school to transform itself into this kind of institution.

Dr. Augusto Cury is the idealizer of the Intelligence School program. We are brought to tears when we see its results in over one hundred thousand students. Dozens of countries are interested in applying this method. Dr. Cury has renounced his copyrights of the E.I. program in Brazil so that it can be made available to public and private schools and offered for free to young people in at risk situations, such as those who live in orphanages. Talk to the principal at your child's school to learn more about the E.I. program. The emotional future of your child is crucial.

To obtain more information and find out which schools have affiliations with the E.I. program, access: www.escoladainteligencia.com.br or call +55 16 3602 9420.

Augusto Cury Institute

The Augusto Cury Institute offers courses on the quality of life, management of thoughts and stress, and emotional and professional excellence, among others, aimed at professionals, educators, parents, and young people. To find out more about this institute and which unit is closest to you, access: www.augustocurycursos.com.br.

Review Request

Before you go, can I ask you for a quick favor?

Would you please leave this book an honest review on Amazon?

Your review won't take long, but it can help this book
reach more readers like you.

Thank you for reading, and thank you so much for
being part of the journey.

-Augusto

www.ingramcontent.com/pod-product-compliance
Lightning Source LLC
Chambersburg PA
CBHW030842090426
42737CB00009B/1075